The Advantage of Disadvantage

Presented by Dr. Ruben West

(With Select Authors)

All rights reserved. No part of this publication may be reproduced, distributed, or transmitted in any form or by any means, including photocopying, recording, or other mechanical methods, without the prior written permission of the publisher, except in the case of brief quotations embodied in critical reviews and certain other noncommercial uses permitted by copyright law.

ISBN-13: 978-1533482549
ISBN-10:1533482543

For permission requests please email the publisher, Info@rubenwest360.com addressed "Attention: Permissions Coordinator."

Ordering information

Quantity Sales. Special discounts are available in quantity purchases by corporations, associations, networking groups. For details contact:

Traci Ward
www.iamenoughtw.com
Traci.ward40@gmail.com
785-554-1841

Dedication

This book is dedicated to my children Monica, Spencer, and Robinson, my wife Robin, my parents Robert and Rosetta, as well as the rest of my family and friends that continue to encourage me. Thank you for your love and support. Never stop pursuing your dreams. To Edwina Blackman, RN; Thank you for speaking life and truth in to me at a time when I needed it most. I listened.

To my close friends, my Black Belt Speaker family, the (G3) Glory Triplets, my Uncle, Bishop Charles L. Byrd, and everyone else who believed and continues to believe that together we can make a difference even one life at a time; this book is for you.

Foreword By: Dr. Ruben West

When you hear the phrase "the Advantage of Disadvantage" it almost seems like an oxymoron. How can being faced with a disadvantage be an advantage? But trust me, it is real. Life is going to throw challenges at us, but our response to those challenges is what gives our life more meaning. This book is filled with stories of people who faced challenges, but who then used them and the disadvantages that came with them, to get the most out of their lives.

Think about it, do you recall ever hearing about a heavyweight boxing champion that grew up with a silver spoon in their mouth? I bet you do not. Most of them grew up in a very difficult environment, facing numerous challenges every day. However, despite the fact that they were placed in difficult situations, they decided that they must fight their way out of it to live the life they desired. They would use their disadvantages to their advantage.

Life gives us setbacks and challenges to see how we will respond. We can give up and decide that there is no hope or we can decide to give it our all and create a way even when there doesn't seem to be one. The truth is, champions are known by their triumphs but they were developed by their trials.

The co-authors within this book did a masterful job at articulating just how tough life can be. Like all of us, they faced difficult times, challenging situations, and unforeseen negative circumstances. There were times that they needed help and felt as though they had no one to assist them. That's when they realized that sometimes the only helping hand you're going to find is at the end of your own wrist.

If you're looking for strategies to overcome life's difficult situations, they are in this book. If you know someone who is facing a difficult time and needs a glimmer of hope, give them this book. If surviving is just not enough and you want to learn steps and strategies to thrive, I urge you to use the ones listed in this book.

If you have challenges in your life just know that they were not put there to stop you, they were put there to bring out the best in you. Join me along with these authors and learn how to use your disadvantages as your advantage.

Table of Contents

Dedication	iii
Foreword By: Dr. Ruben West	v
Becoming Aware through Love, Health and Loss By Lisa Marie Martin	11
Freedom Fighter: Finding Your Freedom Through Forgiveness By Patrick Artis	27
An Unexpected Journey By Monique Tucker	49
Staring Stuttering in the Face By Cicone Prince	83
The Quiet Storm By Dr. Nekeshia C. Doctor	93
A Journey Called Life By Jennifer Tuley	103
Starting Fresh By Gwen Cunningham	127
Activate Your Faith By Shavara Lyons	147
Be True To Yourself By Dr. Felicia Shaw	167

Becoming Aware through Love, Health and Loss

By Lisa Marie Martin

I've always been on a journey to become healthy spiritually, mentally, and physically. I wasn't always good at listening to my body. I'm the person who pushes through - burns the midnight oil so to speak. As I embarked on my spiritual and health journey, I had to learn a few lessons. But before we get into those lessons, let me take you back.

I was adopted as an infant and grew up as an only child. So with that sad, I had no health reference. I have always had an anemia health issue. I remember as a child taking the liquid iron with orange juice. Needless to say, it wasn't very tasty. I would go through my childhood, teen years, and my adult life with this issue. I would continuously go through physicians and physicals with the same diagnosis "low hemoglobin." To attempt to fix the diagnosis, I was put on a regiment of iron supplements, exercising and eating iron rich foods.

Understand despite the diagnosis, I considered myself a fairly high energy person. I was used to compensating for low energy. In high school M&Ms and Pepsi were my best friends. Quick energy, but a quick drop as well. While in college, I attempted to donate blood for extra credit. Of course, one of the criteria for donating is your hemoglobin must be above a 12. Which of course, mine was not.

I went on to join the military, raise twin boys as a single Mom, graduate with a Bachelor's and Master's Degree while working full time. (Trust me, good and bad stress affects your energy level and your mood). During this period, I quit drinking soda (Pepsi was my soda of choice). I discovered sugar and it wasn't a good match either. I didn't care for the constant crashes. I always considered myself health conscious since I was raised in a diabetic family.

Helping my Mom and my Grandmother with their meals gave me conscious eating habits. I remember measuring foods on a scale and ensuring all the food groups were present. Understand not only were Mom and Grandmother diabetic, it ran throughout the family.

At the eight years old I lost my father to multiple myeloma, a disease of the white blood cells. Three months later I lost my Grandfather. I didn't know him well. But I remember two funerals in a short amount of time took a toll on my Mom even though she put up a brave front. She handled both funerals with courage and grace. A year later my aunt Nevada would also pass.

As time went on I would lose my grandmother to colon cancer and my Mom to diabetic complications and two strokes. My parents were both older at the time of my adoption. My immediate family is now deceased, but I have a host of cousins throughout the US. When you lose immediate family through various illnesses, you realize how precious life is.

These events impacted my eating and exercise decisions throughout my life. I knew I didn't want to end up controlling my health by having to stick needles into myself.

As the years progressed, I started looking for ways to increase my energy level due to the low hemoglobin levels. **Vivaren** was my best friend while I took care of my infant sons during the day and worked nights. I had a wake-up call while I was sitting in the hospital with my Mom. I was waiting for the doctor to give me an update on her condition. She was diagnosed with having a stroke. When her doctor came in, he looked at me and said if I didn't slow down and get some real rest he was going to put me on the bed beside her. Fortunately, I ended up seeing my doctor who in no uncertain terms told me I was suffering from exhaustion. So, at this point, *Vivaren* was not my friend because it only masked my symptoms.

The next stage of my health journey began when I moved to Wichita to take another position with the military. I was assigned a new physician who happened to be female. She was not satisfied with my health history of "low hemoglobin". She asked me if I had a history or did my family have a history. I stated, "Unknown" due to being an adoptee.

My new doctor was determined to find a real solution to my problem. After being referred to a hematologist, I came to a new understanding of my diagnosis, Alpha Thalassemia, a blood disorder that reduces the production of hemoglobin. Hemoglobin is the protein in red blood cells that carries oxygen to cells throughout the body. This diagnosis meant I did not process iron like normal individuals. Wow! That explained a lot regarding my previous life/beginnings and struggles with energy. This diagnosis came about in 2006.

I had contemplated for some years whether or not I would take the time to search for my biological parents. This unknown came with all kinds of mixed emotions. I took the leap of faith to say yes. This leap of faith would answer a lot of questions. Finding my biological parents, was a revelation I wished I would have said yes to before now. But God had his own timing. I'm thankful I finally said yes. I found my Mom and in turn my Mom found my Dad (to date, I have only met him via phone).

My biological grandmother was the first to discover I was searching. She said she always knew she would be the first one to know when I would come searching for my Mom. Upon location through a private agency, I was able to reconnect with my Mom. It was a week before I picked up the phone to make the call because I was so nervous. All the "what if's" arose. Even though those doubts came up, I finally picked up the phone to call the number the agency gave me. Unbeknownst to me, she had been sitting by the phone awaiting my call for seven days upon notification. Our conversation was of elation and love. But one of her first questions to me was, "How is your health?" I said, "Fine, I've just been anemic".

I proceeded to give her my diagnosis of Alpha Thalassemia. From that moment on, I came to the realization the "thalassemia" trait ran in our family in various forms. This revelation made me take a stand to take care of myself from the inside out. I wanted to ensure I was able to help myself and others to take care of themselves spiritually, physically, and mentally. Upon this life journey, I started a fitness website

LisasFitnessdreams4u.com. I started this to help empower others as well as myself to take control, exercise, and to improve ourselves.

As I was becoming aware of me, I was not only on a health journey but a continued spiritual mission. Upon meeting my biological Mom, I had many spiritual realizations. Like not knowing how two people could be so inner-connected without ever being in one another's world.

The foundation of God was ingrained in me due to being raised in a Christian family. Prayer in any form whether it was exercised verbally or through writing has been a staple throughout my life. I grew up singing in the youth choir and going to Wednesday night prayer meetings.

When you have experienced an array of religious backgrounds life can become a bit confusing. I would like to share a bit of my religious background for you. I was christened in a Methodist Church as a baby. Baptized in a Baptist church at the age of 6. My Mom was Catholic at one time and joined the Baptist church before my birth. My Grandmother was Jehovah Witness, my Grandfather was a Church of God minister, and my Aunt was Pentecostal. Those are the ones that immediately come to mind. But I'm sure you get the picture.

For me, over time, these various religions brought clarity and oneness. I remember experiencing doubt and questions. I read everything from the Bible, The Course in Miracles, Rumi, Dr. Wayne Dwyer, Iyanla Vanzant, Nelson Mandela, Deepak Chopra, Eckhart Tolle and a host of others. All the nuggets, inspiration, and wisdom I've taken through these wonderful authors has been an experience.

The experiences brought an understanding of the Love and the spiritual realm of God. Of knowing God is within us and surrounds us on a constant basis. The life lessons I've learned along this journey reminds me to always continue to be on the journey. To seek wisdom, guidance, and the Love of God in everything that I am and everything that I will become.

Growing up as a reader, a writer of poems and respect for the written word, allowed my soul to open up to see beyond myself. Reading for me is the ability to travel through the eyes and the heart.

How to Become Aware of You

Upon meeting my biological family, I realized we were all centered in the same thought process. It's not about religion it's about Love. We came from different walks of life, but we had the same purpose, the spiritual journey of Love and of God.

Due to losing loved ones throughout my younger years, holidays, dates, and events were hard. Upon finding my second family, who encompassed and wrapped my family in their loving arms, and accepted us as we were, with all our imperfections (understand, life is a continuous journey). I realized this opportunity was a blessing to my family. We had the love and gift of a second family.

This chapter would be long if I entailed the whole journey of warming up to our new family, learning to open up, learning to be more expressive, and learning to hug with more depth and to listen even more intently to God's purpose and truth. Instead, I'm going to give you some nuggets, inspiration and thoughts on that have helped me to arrive at the above.

What does becoming you mean? Keep in mind, we are a continuous work in progress.

Be your authentic self. No one is "you" and that is your power. We are all different, and that makes each one of us an individual. I have never been one to fall into the in-crowd. Daring to be great and daring to be different is ok. Never underestimate that power. Yes, there will be bumps along the way, but you have to remember to keep your head held high. Change for the right reasons. Change to be more authentic. Change to understand the God within you and the love that surrounds you.

> *"We walk by faith not by sight."*
> 2 Corinthians 5:7

My Mom always reminded me, the little voice inside of you is God speaking to you. I have always lived by that. I like to say, that is God tugging at your heart strings to stop, look, and listen. Perhaps it's a message to move forward with your decision or to proceed with caution. Whatever, the message may be, it behooves you to take the time to be still and listen.

> *"Sleep and dream of joy, and remember above all else: You feel good not because the world is right, but your world is right because you feel good."*
> Dr. Wayne Dyer

This quote can go the distance for so many circumstances in life. For me, it brings me back to the journey. In the last year, I finally found a doctor who could balance my metabolism which has in turn helped my mood, my nutrition, my outlook, and my overall health. When a friend told me about this physician, I went with apprehension. For me, it was important to take this step to get my health on track. Keep in mind, I had been through supplements, iron infusions, low energy days, and an array of vitamins.

Upon examination, I discovered I was on the low end of the Vitamin D spectrum (I work in an office with no windows). That alone can alter your mood. Vitamin D is not something doctors check on a regular basis; therefore, it needs to be requested. Not only was I low on Vitamin D, but I was also low on other nutrients that help stabilize the metabolism as well as keeping weight off.

Since I have been under his care, I have felt a 90-degree turn around from where I started. Even though I thought I was doing everything right, I still had room for improvement. I still had room for knowledge. So, this quote brings my health full circle. When you feel, you can help others, you will know the world is right for that moment in time. You will know you can trust the journey.

Physical Self-Care

> *"You cannot be useful to yourself, others or God if you run yourself ragged. To serve others, support others, give to others, you must first be able to help, support and give to yourself."*
>
> *Iyanla Vanzant*

If you don't love yourself, take care of yourself, and be grateful for what God has given you, you cannot help others the way you were intended to do so. I didn't always do a good job of taking care of myself. I was quick to help others but did not have the foresight to listen to my body. Trust me your body will stop you in your tracks.

I have gone through several bouts of lower back pain from lifting weights wrong or for some unknown reason.

I have often thought to myself after being free of that pain, that I never want to go through that again. I'm sure there were numerous causes for it and things I should have been more aware of.

The long and the short of it is, you must be careful in the things you do. Be conscious of your body, because pain and discomfort are a continuous reminder of what we need to do with health issues that we have at the moment.

Even though pain may knock you down, don't give up. Stay on the path to your health and well-being. Yes, you may have to improvise until that body part gets better. But remember, doing something is better than doing nothing.

Spiritual Self-Care.

"You have to love yourself because no amount of love from others is sufficient to

fill the yearning that your soul requires from you."

Dodinsky

The military tends to make you a morning person. Even though, by nature, I'm not a typical morning person. I love to sleep on the weekends since I do wake up early during the week. But since my metabolism has been running a lot smoother, I have found myself to be a morning person with gratitude.

Don't get me wrong, I'm not ready to talk to anyone until I do the following.

- Give thanks upon waking
- Brush my teeth
- Drink a glass of water
- Move my body whether it's stretching or yoga or even a workout (depending on my schedule, this can occur morning and afternoon. Or only once a day).
- Whatever, the case, doing some form of physical activity will wake your body up and get the organs moving. Your workouts are important meetings you should schedule with yourself. Bosses don't cancel, so why should you.
- Lastly, I have a cup of coffee and eat something that has protein in it to get going.

Smiles and Hugs

Not everyone is a hugger, so the opportunity to hug someone may not present itself. But if that chance should arise, sometimes words are not needed, just a silent of hug will go a long way.

Take the time to smile at least one person a day. You never know, that smile may be a blessing. Besides, it will make your heart smile.

"Gratitude can transform common days into thanksgivings, turn routine jobs into joy, and change ordinary opportunities into Blessings."

William Arthur Ward

I love this quote, because being thankful, having gratitude, and taking the time to speak to God, can make your day brighter. Never be in such a big hurry you're not able to stop and pray with gratitude.

As Iyanla Vanzant states, *"In times when you feel weak and vulnerable, it is easy to lose faith in your ability to go on. It is precisely in these times that you must turn to the infinite power within yourself."*

Always know Prayer can take place anywhere and anytime. Prayer is nothing more than a conversation with God.

Most of my prayers take place in my car when I'm traveling from point A to B.

It's something about seeing the sky and taking in my surroundings those moments in the car can be the most precious ones. And of course, I'm praying for the drivers around me since we live in the electronic age.

I was in St. Port Lucie, Florida this past year. I had finally taken a real vacation where I was able to disconnect from the Blackberry, the laptop, and the constant needs of work. It was a time; I was able to give thanks, to feel God's love through the beauty of nature and to feel the freedom of the beach, the water, and the sky. Disconnecting from your busy life is important to enable you to feel and enjoy the quiet and peaceful moments of God's love and grace.

Be Free As A Butterfly

As I embark on another birthday (the young age of 47), I feel the best is yet to come. As I bring my thoughts to a close. I want to leave you with the meaning of butterflies as expressed by my family.

- Butterflies are free. They have an internal guidance system to always help them find their way!

- They make their home among the flowers and drink sweet nectar as they share and spread their pollen of nourishment and joy to others.

- Butterflies are Beautiful. They have come through an amazing altering transformation.

- They have "imaginal cells" which turn their former bodies into a new form that can fly instead of crawl.

- The Butterfly trusts all things, allows all things and thereby transcends all things.

- This is also what Love does.

- May you be inspired to be like a Butterfly and Soar!

- Live Your Best Life!

The dreams and goals of yesterday are today's goals and tomorrow's successes.

Love and Blessings Always, Lisa

About Lisa Martin

Lisa Martin was born and raised in Topeka, KS. She has adult twin sons as well as a granddaughter. Currently, Lisa is full time with the Kansas Army National Guard. She is also an adjunct professor at Baker University, a fitness and health coach, mentor and Vice President for a non-profit program called STEPS (Students Trained to Excel with Purpose for Success). Lisa graduated from Washburn University with a degree in Public Administration, and she is also a graduate of Baker University with a Masters in Management.

Lisa enjoys helping others to become aware of their fitness and health goals as well as their inner self. Her desire is to inspire others to dig deep and to be the best person they can be physical, mentally, and spiritually. Lisa's motto is: The dreams of yesterday are today's goals and tomorrow's successes. Lisa's contact information is:

lisasdreams4u@gmail.com

www.facebook.com/lisa.marie.martin

www.facebook.com/LisasFitnessDreams4U

Freedom Fighter: Finding Your Freedom Through Forgiveness

By Patrick Artis

"The truth is, unless you let go, unless you forgive yourself, unless you forgive the situation, unless you realize that the situation is over, you cannot move forward."

Steve Maraboli

In The Beginning…

Children are like a sponge, they soak up everything, so much so that it may take years to wash away the negative stains left on their young minds and sometimes, those stains never go away. Growing up in a single parent home was everything but easy. According to the U.S. Census Bureau, in 2014 there were 3 out of 12 million single parent families and 80% of those were headed by single mothers. Today 1 in 4 children under the age of 18, a total of about 17.4 million, are being raised without a father and nearly half live below the poverty line. My childhood was no exception to this horrible statistic. My mother worked two jobs and sometimes a third, all at the same time, just to provide for my sister and I.

Doing the best that she knew, she sacrificed so much and sometimes even that was not enough to make ends meet. I was a very curious and an observant child growing up. I would constantly think to myself, "why does my lovely mother always talk about robbing people?". I would hear her say to us, "Now baby, this week is going to be a little tight again because I have to rob Peter to pay Paul". (Robbing Peter to pay Paul is a colloquialism, meaning a person has to sacrifice paying one bill to have enough money to pay another). I remember hearing my mother talk as if they were real, along with "Mr. Bill" and "Uncle Sam". I would often wonder who were they and how come they never stopped by? But little did I know, they would pay us a visit, faithfully every month.

I would think to myself, "how come the police aren't looking for my mother by now with all this robbing?" These tough moments seemed to become the norm, rather than the exception. It was the way of life as we knew it and would have a compound effect later in my life. I could see the effects of this lifestyle causing my family unneeded internal stress that had visible outward effects.

My mother's cigarette smoking increased from one to two packs a day; my sister had to sacrifice her adolescent years to help support the house at the age of thirteen, and I witnessed first-hand just how cruel kids could be as they picked on me because of the type of clothes I wore. My mother would often make my clothes because we could not afford to go shopping in the department stores all the time.

I remember in the late 80's when I was in the third grade, my mother made me a pair of MC Hammer pants. They were plaid print; burgundy with gold, brown, and black stripes. We could not afford the Patent Leather shoes that everyone else wore, so my mother told me to make do with what I had and I pulled the Penny Loafers out of the closet. My mother knew how to package a lesson within any situation during this time. Like my first lesson on my worth and values as she expressed, *"nobody's name or clothes is better than your own, know your worth"*.

In spite of the hard times, with my S-Curl complementing my flattop haircut, I thought I was MC Hammer himself, until I got to school where the kids brought me back to reality. My clothes would often carry a head jerking stench from the kerosene heater we used to heat the house or boil water to take a bath. Struggling with bills and life's curve balls was the primary focus and topic of discussion every month, because it was what we talked about, it became what we brought about. Remember, what you focus on expands in your life.

The seed of resentment and anger was beginning to germinate inside of me like wild crabgrass growing in a garden. These were the first moments that my mental programming was being influenced by my reality. Secretly dealing with the struggle to fit in, I would find myself socially aloof at times, lacking the communication skills to connect with people because of statements that were repeated to me as a child. Have you ever heard the saying, children are to be seen and not heard? These words were branded on my brain as a child, because of that, I didn't talk much. The lack of confidence and ability to communicate effectively would haunt me into my adult years, which lead to many missed opportunities later in life.

You can say that I was clearly facing a disadvantage. Can you think of an unfortunate circumstance that occurred during your childhood that stuck with you throughout your adult years? Did you have any resentment towards the person or situation? How did you deal with it? I will give you steps on how to positively answer these questions a little later.

The Struggle From Within

I remember one of my favorite Christmas'. It was the late 80's. I finally got the blue and white BMX bike that I had been wanting for months! One would think that we had a planned family gathering at my Aunt Martha's house, but unfortunately, that was not the case. This Christmas was spent at my aunt's house because this time, my mother had to "rob" both Peter and Paul and our electricity was disconnected two days prior to Christmas. To make matters worse, our water was shut off and the pipes froze. I was secretly wondering, "where was the man who would show up periodically and call himself my father? I mean, we looked just alike, so how come you would not want your child to spend Christmas in their own home?

Doesn't your love for us last longer than the short moments you spend with us while you're in town? Or does your "unanchored" love fade away like the exhaust fumes from your tailpipe as you drive away waving your goodbyes?" Both are toxic and deadly if consumed for an extended period of time. These were the thoughts that were taking up real estate inside of my head as a child. My life was becoming a series of unanswered questions, but as the youngest, I was too shy to speak up. Have you ever had a moment where you felt lost? Or maybe something did not feel quite right to you, but you did not say anything at the time?

This would explain where I was during this period. How could my mother let this happen to us?

There is an African proverb that says, *"If there is no enemy within, the enemy outside can do us no harm."* And the "enemy" of confusion, conflict, chaos, and insecurity was growing rapidly inside of me like an Arizona wildfire in the middle of summer. Like many people today, the conflict was internal and I did not know how to handle it other than lashing out. I would hang around the wrong crowd, sacrificing my family morals just to be accepted, because home was where the struggle was and I did not want to be a part of it. I found it convenient to place blame on my mother since she was the one consistently present in my life. It wasn't until after I was older that I realized the pressures that single mothers go through – always the scapegoat for an absent father. After all, out-of-sight, out-of-mind right? And for this Christmas, like many others, my father was (AWOL) Absent and Without Love.

He was absent and so was his love. So I can only imagine my mother's embarrassment at the lack of electricity and water, but I guess she figured that the happiness of her children was far more valuable than that of her feelings. This was the power and strength my mother possessed, because like magic, she tried her best to make us feel like we were doing better than what we really were. Instead of Houdini, I sometimes call her

"Herdini" from the many "rabbits" she was able to pull out of her preverbal hat. David Blaine has nothing on Willie Mae Artis! She was determined to not let her lack keep her from making that day special for her children.

Engulfed with a strong sense of work ethic that was handed down from my late grandfather, my mother knew how to make lemonade from the lemons life handed her. So the question would often cross my mind, how could a woman raise a son and teach him how to be a man? The short answer is, contrary to popular belief, a woman cannot raise a son to be a man. I know my answer may not be the most popular amongst some single mothers, but women are not equipped to do so.

She could not play catch with me, teach me how to change the oil in my car, or have the man-to-man moments that made a father special in a son's eyes. My mother did all that she could and well, the rest, she did what Mother Teresa said, and allowed me to become "a pencil in the hands of God". So to every woman who may be tasked with raising a child alone, then hear this from me: you can do all things through God who gives you strength, and for everything else, leave it up to Him to work out.

This is what my mother did. But often times, it was not enough – something was missing. Have you ever felt like you were the only one going through a situation and everyone else was going through life just fine leaving you thinking, what's wrong with me? God, did you slight me of a chromosome or two? Why does it seem as if I'm drowning in the very things that others are walking on top of?

Have you ever tasted a food dish, and you tried to put your finger on what was in it, but you could not figure out what that missing ingredient was? Well, for most of my life, this described how I felt every time I looked in the mirror staring at a lost reflection gazing back at me. And that missing ingredient was the presence of my father. See as a child, my father would come around just long enough to leave me haunted by cliffhanger thoughts floating in my head, promising that he'd be back for good. The sporadic presence of my father created a stain of instability and insecurity that lead to many failed relationships that haunted me for years.

As a side note, parents understand that no matter how many times you may tell your children something, do not be surprised when their actions lineup more with your actions than your words.

Children are visual learners. They do not have previous experiences to reference so they do what they see verses what they are told. This holds true for many adults as well. Be mindful of your actions, as parents, authority figures, and leaders, make sure that those actions are in line with the words that you speak.

Someone is always watching. And as a child, I was watching everything my father and mother were or were not doing. The absence of my father's presence and the structure and direction that a father gives helped to shape my reality, and thus my "norm".

Lost G.P.S.

They say "if you want to make God laugh, tell Him your plans." Many of us go through life thinking we have everything mapped out and all we have to do is just live life according to "our" plan. But God sometimes has other plans for us. Similar to Denver Broncos Quarterback Peyton Manning shouting out "Omaha!" "Omaha!" – his signal that he's changing a play right before the ball is snapped – the Creator called an audible tailor-made just for me. It was late one evening, I was returning home from hanging with some friends. I received a voice mail from my brother David Jr, telling me that he had bad news. With shakiness in his voice, he slowly uttered out, "he's gone. Dad is gone."

As I listened to the recording over and over in disbelief, I could do nothing but stand in my bedroom stunned. Finally, when things began to make sense and I had begun the process of forgiving my father, I am hit in the face by the messenger of misery. I had a pastor that would always say, "Life has a way of flipping on you." I am reminded of a quote that says, "Holding someone in unforgiveness, is like drinking poison and wishing the other person would die." The irony of this quote was it was not just an analogy, but it was my reality.

My father was gone and I felt as if there was no hope of reconciling. In that moment, it was as if life had been sucked out of me and I was devastated. My anger grew out of hopelessness and I pointed my anguish towards God. During times of reflection I would often wonder why God would allow such a tragedy to happen to me at this stage of my life. There I was, seventeen, and still grieving over the passing of my grandfather who had made his transition three months prior, standing in dismay, in the doorway of my room. I was at a loss for words.

The only thing I could think of was, "who was going to tell me who I was now? Who was going to define me? Where did my last name, Artis, come from and what do we stand for?" It's in our fathers, who give us our identity. A father is like a GPS (Global Positioning System) constantly giving a child direction and sometimes correcting them by rerouting their positioning when needed. "My "GPS" is gone forever" was the stabbing thought that pierced my soul. My father passed away at the early age of fifty-six, leaving a trail of tears and unanswered questions that created a huge crater in my spiritual DNA. The seeds planted from my childhood insecurities were now germinating and I quickly was filled with an internal rage that left me seeing relationships as worthless as gold-plated jewelry. I would create a "shiny" atmosphere, but would keep people at a distance for fear that they would see the pain from my past. I found a comfort in showing people what I thought they wanted to see. This mindset created a series of shallow relationships that ended prematurely as soon as I felt internally threatened.

The answer to filling the huge void left by my father came in the form of short physical relationships with women that created an even larger gap in my ability to connect with people. I mean after all, I had first-hand knowledge of showing people what "unanchored" unattached love looked like from growing up and seeing it as a child. Again, people do what they see when they have no previous reference point or experience. What I saw was how I could not trust people, let alone love people because I was struggling with loving myself. This would further impact the relationships I had. I am not claiming to give my father all of the credit for how I may have mismanaged relationships, but not having a "life GPS" present early in my life, only left me feeling my way around with my eyes wide shut.

My life was filled with a lot of trials and even more errors. I would find myself searching for mentors to fill the void, and often times, temporarily attaching myself to male figures I adopted as unwitting role models. My choices would sometimes backfire from receiving advice that was not in line with my morals or values. But desperate people do desperate things. Or as the old saying goes, "you will fall for anything if you don't stand for something." The struggle of not having a "life GPS" can leave you accepting direction from many different sources, which will lead you to many different decisions.

This is a problem I see in today's society. Many people are getting advice from all over the place and ultimately it leaves them, all over the place. They are the busy, but unproductive people who are left feeling lost and unfulfilled. It took me 11years to realize that it was not all my father's fault, nor my mother's, but in life, we all have our "hand" that we're dealt. As Kenny Rogers famously put it in his song, "The Gambler", we must know when to hold 'em and know when to fold 'em. We have to know whose advice to keep and whose advice to discard.

Another issue I was having is not so different from the issues that many others face today. I was placing all the blame on everyone and everything else and not taking responsibility for my part. Unfortunately, many people are not willing to participate in their own rescue in life. Take a second to think of someone you may know who fits that description. Don't be surprised if that person you think of is the one reading this book right now.

For the first time in my life, I realized that I was having a true struggle with the experiences I had growing up, and it came well packaged in the emotion of unforgiveness. This condition is like a cancer that will metastasize quickly in your mind and ultimately settle in your heart.

Inside Job: The Road to Redemption

The word redeem is defined as *"the action of regaining or gaining possession of something in exchange for something."* After feeling like I was an extra in the movie "Groundhog Day", I got tired of rehearsing the same things year over and over and not being fulfilled. Regardless of what I tried, I would end up with the same results. This was largely because my mind was stuck in a loop filled with anger and hopelessness through my unforgiveness. I did what the Prodigal Son in the Bible did, and "came to myself," or you can say I had a moment of clarity. Just like when he found himself inside of a pigpen, he took assessment and probably said, *"What am I doing"? I was created for more than this. This has got to end today!"*

Can you think of a time that you got to the point where you had a moment of being sick and tired of being sick and tired of something? That moment could be a broken relationship, a lack of finances, or just being in your own way of living the life you deserve. I remember my moment it like it was yesterday. I was sick and tired of being held a prisoner to my past and was in search of my very own emancipation.

My "pigpen" came in the form of unforgiveness, lack of direction, focus, and faith from a disadvantaged childhood. It was messy and I was looking for a way out. This was when I recalled the words that my mother graciously said to me as a nine year old little boy, *"no one else's name is better than your own - know your worth."*

I took a deep breath and made a decision to exhale the moments of misery, madness, and mediocrity that I was allowing to control me for so long. Yes, it was me allowing this to happen to me. I had to be my own rescue because no one else was coming. It was time to resuscitate the potential that was dying inside of me for so long. If you're taking notes, write down the word ***decision*** and ***action.***

Call to Action

The first lesson I learned was that I had to make a decision to take action. A decision to not act is still a decision being made, and nothing happens if you do nothing. That was the moment when I looked at my life and believed that there was more to living than what I went through as a child. They say that most people "die" at the age of twenty-one but they aren't buried until they reach their seventies and eighties. In other words, there are many people who fall victim to the "walking" dead syndrome. They would allow the shortfalls, their environment, or insufficiencies keep them captive for the rest of their life.

They would keep that part of their life alive by packaging it in mediocrity and ultimately becoming addicted to powerlessness. So I made the decision to not let this become my story. Think of a time when you know you needed to make a change for the better, but for some reason you were in the same place a month later, six months later, or even years later.

Maybe you talked about it so much, that people were tired of having the same old conversation. Or maybe you were like me, so good at giving lackluster excuses, that your excuses had excuses. I would get upset when confronted by a real friend who called me out on it.

I grew uncomfortable around them, because I knew deep down that I actually wanted better for myself. Can you relate? There is a story about a dog that kept howling over and over so loudly that it caused a man to ask the owner of the dog, what was wrong? The owner replied and said that the dog was lying on a nail. The neighbor said, "Well, why doesn't he move?" The owner cleverly answered saying, "I guess it's not hurting him bad enough." That was my story for so long. "It" was not hurting bad enough for me to take action. Maybe this is you as well?

Think about something that you have been talking about doing, for so long, but just have not done anything about it. It could be, because, it's not hurting you bad enough. Until the pain of staying the same becomes greater than the pain of change, then you will never change. Are you ready to make a decision to act now?

Write down at least three things that you want to accomplish within the next six months.

Three things to accomplish within 6 months:

1._____

2._____

3._____

The Power of Perspective

After seeing my life leading to a dead end very quickly, I had to change how I saw things. Remember, that once you change your focus, you change your future. When I chose to give my perspective a makeover, life took on a brand new meaning. I took an assessment of the things that I went through as a child, and wrote them down. As I wrote, I began to realize that without those moments, life would have been boring and mundane. It would have looked like a flat line, instead of vertical jagged edges filled with peaks and valleys. It was in those "valley" moments that gave the peaks so much power that lead me to my purpose of sharing my story because I realized that I was not in this fight alone.

Once I thought about those moments, it fed a different side of my perspective that gave me life again. I realized that life was not about avoiding the storms, but learning how to dance in the rain. And it was during the "rainy" seasons that I survived, that stimulated my growth spiritually, physically, and emotionally. I invite you to do the same. I had developed a strong appreciation for those trying moments life handed me while I was growing up. With this new vision, it set in motion a rebirth of who I was to become and began to be the antidote for overcoming the unforgiveness towards my father that I carried for so long.

Right now take an account of those painful moments that you went through, and take note that you survived it just to bear witness of how things turned around for you. This is your peak moment.

Once I centered my focused on the outcome I desired instead of the moment of despair, my thoughts began to change for the better. Remember what I said before? You get what you focus on, and this holds true for everything in life. Or as my pastor says, "Thoughts become things, if not interrupted." So focus on the outcome you are expecting instead of what you are currently facing and you will start to see life unfolding before your eyes. Take a moment and write down your "valley" moments and your "peak" moments.

Your Valley Moments:

_____

_____

Your Peak Moments:

_____

_____

Seeing is Believing

Lesson number three for you note takers would be change your perspective. There was a movie that came out in 2008 called "Vantage Point" starring Dennis Quaid and Forest Whitaker. Without giving too much of the movie away, it was about a series of people who witnessed an incident from different vantage points. Everyone who gave their account of what happened was absolutely correct based on how they saw the event.

The point I'm making to you is, if you are finding yourself in situations that don't serve you, then you may need to change your *vantage point.* Today, I help to show people how changing their story and their limited thinking can take on a light that delivers hope and helps to empower them to step into a better version of themselves. It was **Socrates** that stated, ***"Whether if you think you can or if you think you can't, either way, you are right."*** Life as you know it is based on your ability to believe.

I realized that my value was wrapped up in my belief that I had about myself. It wasn't until that moment when I remembered my mother telling me that **"nobody's name is more valuable than my own",** that I really believed it. Have you ever got to the point with the life you were living that enough was enough? Or maybe a relationship that you would hope change for the better, only got worse? You realize that your value is worth more than the "victim" status that you found comfort in from time to time.

It was **Martin Luther King Jr.** who said, that *"Freedom isn't given by the oppressor, but it must be demanded by the oppressed."* It's that moment when you realize that your freedom is connected to your faith, forgiveness, and your willingness to fight for the life that you deserve.

As I look back now, it was in the many turbulent times growing up as a child, that empowered me to be able to serve in the capacity that I do today. It was during those times, of seeing my mother struggle, fighting internal anger, and dealing with the weight of unforgiveness, that gave me the strength and resiliency to encourage the youth of today, to give them a sense of hope for tomorrow.

This is the essence of the brand Gladiators. This is what it means to fight for the life you deserve, build relationships of quality, and become non-negotiable about your goals and dreams as it all serves your purpose to be free to live your best life now.

About Patrick Artis

Patrick Artis is an electrifying motivational speaker who believes in the core value he learned while in the Air Force, and that is "SERVICE BEFORE SELF." It was from the sixteen plus years of him serving his country that fueled Patrick's passion to serve in a different capacity outside of the military. Understanding that we are all fighting for what we want, because if not, then what we do not want will take over. It was in that moment that Patrick founded the Gladiators International brand, coining the phrases: #WeFight #WeBuild #WeWin.

Patrick uses this platform to inspire and serve youth who, just like him, grew up in search of direction and hope. Patrick has created a movement that empowers the youth to be non-negotiable about their goals and dreams and that all things are possible. Patrick is committed to creating a mindset that establishes a strong vision and teaches principles that delivers hope and limitless possibilities.

He believes in the late Whitney Houston's popular song, "The Greatest Love of All" when she said, "I Believe the Children are the Future", which is why he volunteers his time with the youth, and money through Gifted Gladiators, a scholarship program created, to help supplement tuition for underprivileged youth.

patrick.artis79@gmail.com

An Unexpected Journey

By Monique Tucker

Have you ever reflected over your life and felt disappointment because the hopes, dreams and aspirations that you had for yourself had not happened yet? Perhaps you have attempted to start a project or had an idea to move to an area that would allow you to start your own business, only to become distracted. Maybe through no fault of your own, life just seemed to happen, and not in the way that you had planned. Well, what if I told YOU that YOU can still create the life that you want for yourself? It is not too late! Regardless of your age and stage in life, whether you are in your 20's, 30's, 40's, 50's or beyond, it is never too late to begin again.

You Can Begin Again

If you are reading this book, it is because you have determined that you are fed up with mediocrity, and that you are tired of more of the same, mundane, unfilled living that you have become accustomed to. You have decided that you want to stop being more than just an observer, and become actively engaged in this thing called life. YOUR LIFE. Perhaps you have a desire to start your own business, or maybe you desire to become the best person that you can be. When you realize that the life that you are currently living is very different from the vision that God showed you, or certainly not the life that you would have chosen for yourself, **YOU CHANGE IT!**

My life has been anything but boring, or easy. I was born into a middle class, educated, two parent family household. I am the younger of two siblings; my brother is almost five years older than I. I knew from an early age of about five or six that I was destined to become a motivational speaker. That was the age of the first vision where God showed me on a stage speaking to hundreds of people.

God gave me the vision, but I chose to push it to the back of my mind because I could not see that for myself. It was but a mere dream, and that dream did not fit within the 9 to 5 scope of what seemed acceptable or realistic in my family. It also did not seem to be a real plausible opportunity to make a good living, or at least this is what I believed that my family would think. I considered career fields like teaching, psychology, nursing, social work, and business and even began taking classes for some of them. I even remember entertaining the idea for a long time of being a lawyer just like my father.

Through a series of life experiences, and my desire to empower and change the lives of others, I opted for the career path of social work. I attended the University of Missouri-St. Louis where I graduated with my Bachelor of Social Work degree. This field was the closest thing that I could connect with what my purpose here on earth was to be which is to inspire, empower and motivate others to make life changing decisions that would enable them to live out their life's purpose.

I will tell you now that this was a safe choice for me because I also realized that I had an enormous fear of public speaking, and I avoided any opportunity that required me to have to do this for as long as I possibly could. Disclosing this will be surprising to some people that know me because of my out-going and very bubbly personality.

I expected my life to be successful based on a prescribed set of rules, and I believed that I followed all of the "rules" that my family had ingrained in me. The blueprint that they gave me was that life would go well if I got a good education and worked hard. My father would often say, "the sky is the limit for you, Monique".

I believed that there was nothing that I could not accomplish if I set my mind to it. I was that girl that played by the rules. I was confident, strong minded and ready to conquer the world. I felt unstoppable. I bet you had a similar plan as well. You were working on that business plan when the loan fell through, or maybe the person that you thought that you would spend the rest of your life with walked out after 15 years.

Maybe you have the child that is out of control and you are at your wits end because you have invested all of your time, money and energy and you are ready to give up. Maybe you are sick and tired of being sick and tired and you want something to change.

I believed that my life had fallen into place. Beloved, I want you to take my hand and walk through my journey with me. I want you to feel how I felt as I share with you.

I married my husband when I was twenty-three. I had my expectations, interests and desires, and he had his. We are both good people, but in doing our own reflection on things, realized that our hearts were very different; not to mention our aspirations and direction for our lives. We were also the youngest in our family lines, which meant that he was used to getting his way, and I was used to getting mine. Through our union, we created a beautiful daughter, who is the second love of my life after God.

Not many people will be as candid about their experience as I am going to be, but there were many times where I was both living to die, and dying to live. Who knew that I would lose my sense of self and who I knew God created me to be? Who knew that I would have to do the work to find my way back?

People often stay in situations or experiences longer than they really should. Some people use finances as an excuse to remain, others use children, or the fear of being another statistic, but in some cases, it is the fear of being alone.

When I got married, I married my friend. He was tall, dark and extremely handsome. He made me laugh. He had the values and character traits that I valued, and most importantly, he was a Christian man. We dated for 3 years, and it was good. As a matter of fact, it was great. When we were not in class, and I was not working, we spent many hours together. We did very few things apart.

He was different from anyone that I had dated previously, he was kind, respectful, loved his mother, and closed and opened doors for me. His heart seemed very genuine. During our 3 year courtship, I had learned to love him. I will admit that I was torn between my head and my heart, but nonetheless, I loved him. I believed that based on our courtship, we could have a good, sustainable marriage, so I married him.

The honeymoon period was short to say the least. Things began to change in a matter of weeks. It no longer seemed to be convenient to meet each other for breakfast. The time that we spent at home, we spent in separate rooms. I watched television, and he played his games. One of his nephews unexpectedly lost his father to death, another nephew's parents were divorcing and so my husband, stepped in as the father figure role.

He started spending more time with his nephews, and figured that I would understand. His family began to say things to him after a while because he was gone more than he was at home. We would do the occasional dinner or movie and then go to sleep. I wanted to be sympathetic and understanding. I would expect him to be gone for a few hours a week, and then come home and we have our time. I understood the situation. I recognized that his nephews needed him, he was an amazing uncle, but I also needed my husband.

Month after month, day in and day out, he was gone and so I would spend time with my mother and family. My mother would comment on how her phone would never ring until I left the house. She was right. We tested it.

I could be at home for several hours, and my husband not call me, but if he knew that I was leaving the house, he would call to see what I was doing or ask me when I would be returning home.

I began to feel very alone, and extremely sad. I would find myself crying at different times of the day. If he was home and playing his game, I would be on the couch crying, and wondering what was wrong with me. As time went on, I began to believe that I had made a huge mistake by marrying him. My personal life did not look at all like what I believed that it should have.

Is there a time in your life when you felt disappointed because your plans did not work out the way that you had hoped? You may be sitting here in the exact or similar situation right now. You are probably asking yourself how you got yourself in this situation. You are just like me, right? You had a plan.

You've done everything right, but you find yourself stuck in a rut, and questioning your every decision. Wondering why things are not turning out like you expected. You put the time in, and have given it your all. Why isn't it working? Yeah, I understand and certainly can relate. I asked myself the exact same questions.

When he took breaks from his game, he would check on me to see what I was doing, and I would wipe my eyes and pretend as though everything were okay. He could tell that I was not okay.

We would talk about my feelings, and he would express his. I wanted to be the supportive wife. After all, this was a good man, who worked and then wanted to be there for his nephews. I asked myself how I could be so selfish.

Time To Get Real

I want you to stop right now and think about your life. What needs or areas in your life are being neglected, or would you like to change and how is this impacting you? Write them down.

_____

_____

_____

_____

This process in my life would continue to go on, and he would make some time for me. A dinner date or a movie, and this would be the routine every three or four weeks...sometimes longer. We did get together with friends on occasion, and that would help. I would find myself paying attention to how the other couples related to each other, as I attempted to hide being less than satisfied in my own marriage.

After all, we were supposed to still be newlyweds. We were only a few months into our marriage, and the way we related seemed odd. We did not make time to connect, and he realized that things seemed different and they were. I began to question my decision to get married.

I spent countless hours trying to make sense of my situation. I started questioning who I married, and I remembered feeling that I wanted out. Over time, tensions would rise and I remember arguing with him, and then taking my things and going back to my mother's house for the weekend.

I would like to ask you was there ever a time when you felt like giving up and walking away from something or someone? What kept you from giving up?

My husband would use this opportunity to want to talk, and do whatever I wanted to do. It was the most frustrating thing in the world to me. I felt and it seemed like the only way to get his attention would be to leave.

I would tell him how hurt and alone I felt, and how this was not how I envisioned our marriage. We would talk things through and he would agree to work on the marriage, and I would return back home.

Time To Get Real

What excuses have you made to justify staying in the situation? Write down at least 3.

1. _____

2. _____

3. _____

We started marriage counseling. This process was extremely frustrating and at the same time, insightful for me. I would learn information during one of our marriage sessions that would change my heart toward him, and yet, would help me understand why our dating relationship was so drastically different from our marriage. He admitted to me that he did the things that he believed that I wanted him to do while we were dating, but that since we were married, he wanted me to love him for him, and so basically he did not like really doing a lot of the things that we had done while dating.

As a matter of fact, he seemingly just went along for the ride. My heart sank when I heard this because I felt lied to and betrayed. Initially, I believed that the man that I dated and the man that I married were the same person. The man that I dated and learned to love bought me roses for no reason, took me to dinner, went to concerts, and took me for romantic walks in the park regularly. As a married couple, these things were done very far and few times in between. I realized at that moment that I did not know who I married and this devastated me, but we continued the marriage.

Marriage counseling really seemed to help, but as I reflect now, I realize that it gives some people the ability to be able to complete to do lists, so that they can say that they have done something. Things were better for a while, and we were able to make it through our first year of marriage.

It was our one-year anniversary. We went up to the Lake of the Ozarks. It was during this weekend that my husband expressed wanting to start a family. We had the conversation at dinner, and had an eventful evening which would lead to me getting pregnant with our daughter. I did not realize that I could get pregnant so quickly. I figured that I would have more time.

I was not quite clear on how I felt about so many things. Our relationship was being worked on, and quite frankly, I had just begun trying to get to know the actual person that I did marry. Shortly before finding out that I was pregnant, I had decided to leave my full-time position as a social worker, and took some time off to figure out my next plans.

Finding out that I was pregnant overwhelmed me with a lot of emotions. I had not completely resigned myself to the fact that I was staying in my marriage, but after finding out that I was expecting, I made my decision. I called my husband at work to tell him the wonderful news about me being pregnant, and I pushed any other feelings to the contrary away.

For the next few months ... morning ... afternoon ... and night I was very sick.

I was not working and still had financial obligations. It was a different space for me to be in because I had always had a job since I was fifteen and a half, and now I really had to rely on my husband because we no longer had two incomes. This level of vulnerability was hard. Relationship issues began to surface again. There was an incident at the apartment complex that we lived in, and so we decided to move in with his mother until we got our own place.

I was grateful to feel safe, but that was a less than ideal situation. My husband worked different shifts, and this arrangement worked in case I need someone. I was grateful for the fact that he provided for the both of us, but his views on certain things became very evident. I cannot explain his thought processes nor do I believe that he meant to come across the way that he did at times. Maybe he did. Only he knows. He would share conversations with me about what guys would say about marriage. They were very negative.

These negative views and comments would show up in our marital experiences. It would eventually lead to a power struggle between he and I. He made the money, so I was expected to do what he asked. He was the head of the household so I was supposed to do what he asked. Somehow and at some time, I had become the less than ideal wife. At least this is how I felt.

No matter what I did, it was not good enough. Anything that brought me joy and laughter was silly. I was not brought up on this creed. My household experience between my parents was equal. My dad made more money than my mother did because he was a lawyer, but we never knew it until I was in college. My father and mother raised us to do chores equally and so our experiences were different.

My husband never got the blessing and lesson of giving me time to work through my feelings, so that we could come together as a couple and talk through things. We had another argument, and I left and moved home my mother. I was about four or five months pregnant. I was angry, becoming bitter and tired and still very much lonely. There were many people who talked with us at different times. They were trying to get us back together. I had kept so much from my family with the exception of my mother because I needed some place to go.

My father flew home from Atlanta. I cried because I hated my life, and yet, I was trying to have a healthy pregnancy. I was afraid of being alone even though I had been already. I was afraid of raising a child by myself. I found myself pregnant, jobless, and needing direction. My family helped me, as I decided what to do about my marriage. My husband and I talked, and he asked for another chance. We did love each other after all, so I went along.

We started having some date nights, and I began looking for a job. His family talked with him about me being able to enjoy this pregnancy, and so he and I agreed that I would not work until after our daughter was born. We went apartment hunting, signed the lease and his family moved all of our stuff in. Things seemed better for a time. The baby and I were doing well. I had started gaining weight, and felt good.

Having my daughter was the happiest day of my life. I realized that I truly fell in love when I saw her. She was beautiful. I remember the day of her birth as though it was yesterday. We were both happy. Love felt different to me on a level that I had never experienced before. She was perfect.

My husband and I seemed to be moving forward. He worked, and I was at home for five weeks with her until I started another job. We took shifts so that I could get a nap, and be awake with her as I needed to. He was more helpful, and I appreciated it. All of us got on a schedule, and I went back to work. My daughter stayed with family for a bit during the day until we enrolled her at a day care owned by a family friend. My husband would pick her up, and then go to his mother's house and play games with his nephews. He would stay for hours and then come home.

There were times when we would go home at the same time, and me and the baby would be in the living room, and he would sleep or play his games. Patterns began to surface again, and we slowly started drifting apart. It was like two roommates living together. We would have disagreements on how I would need to change things, and how he missed the connectedness. I would try to conform, and would ultimately lose myself in doing so. This would begin a constant pattern of behavior throughout our six year marriage.

My self-esteem began to take a serious hit. I can remember my husband making comments about things, or not acknowledging any of my efforts. One particular event comes to mind when his family was paying me a visit. He had come home from work, and the house was clean and the refrigerator was cleaned out. This was not an uncommon thing; however, he thanked his mother for doing it. I was appalled. She told him that she did not do it, I did and he said nothing. I still do not know why he thought she would have.

There would also be times when I would ask him if he missed me, and he would reply that he had not thought about it. The truth is, he never thought about it, until and unless, I left him. My father would call, and my husband would always be gone.

My mother would come over, or my best friend at the time, and that would be my entertainment. I remember thinking to myself that one of two scenarios would most likely play out. I would either leave him for good, and/or that he had better hope that no one else showed me attention because he would have something to worry about.

It became clear to me that I was no longer the only one who realized that my marriage was less than perfect. I had been living a lie for a long time, and hiding it.

I would call my father to talk with him about different things that were on my mind. Hurtful things my husband said to me or the emotional abuse that I was suffering. I remember my mother calling to talk to me, and I remember crying because I knew that I could not hold things in anymore. Things had been obvious to my family well before I ever said anything. My husband and I had gotten to the place where I asked to make plans for us, and he agreed. I would make the plans, he would get mad at me, and want to cancel, and so I would leave without him.

I would describe this as a very grueling, depressing and frustrating period of time for me. Mentally and emotionally, I had checked out. I was only present physically until I could find the courage to leave.

Here I was living in a lie. I remember thinking to myself at one point that death had to be better than this. ***The worst lie that you could ever tell is the lie that you tell yourself.*** I was in a very dark place for a time. It was in this space, where I began working on myself. I was living in a lie, but I realized that there were positive things that I could focus on until I was ready to leave.

I had to find ways to build myself up. ***Affirm yourself until you have found a supportive group of people who can help build you up.*** I began to exercise, read positive books, and started spending more time in activities that made me feel good and people whom I believed valued me. Iyanla Vanzant and Joyce Meyers were my saving grace at times, as I watched their television shows each day. Every time I felt negative, I began to tell myself, "Monique, you are fearfully and wonderfully made girl, now start walking in your greatness". ***Start reaching out to people who can help***

support and affirm you. I began finding people that I knew would affirm me, when I did not have the strength at times to affirm myself.

Time To Get Real

Write down at least one actionable item that you can complete this week, and indicate how you intend to accomplish it.

_____

_____

_____

_____

Describe in a few words how you will feel after completing this goal.

_____

_____

_____

_____

I also decided that I wanted to enroll in graduate school. I applied for the graduate MBA program through Lindenwood University. I felt good about this and was excited. I went home and told my husband and he said nothing. A few weeks later, I received my acceptance letter in the mail. I went downstairs in the basement and called my father and mother and they were elated. I already knew that my husband would not be happy for me, but I went upstairs to tell him anyway. As I walked up the stairs, I felt anxious, sad and happy all at the same time. My stomach was in knots though.

As I approached the top of the basement stairs and opened the door, there he was sitting on the couch watching television. He heard me coming up and looked at me. I told him that I had received my acceptance letter into the program. He said nothing. I went into our bedroom just to breathe because I knew that he was not happy for me. He came into the bedroom where I was and said, "Congratulations". I thanked him and that was it.

Over the next few days, we would share the news with his family. Their reaction was mixed as they looked at him and looked at me. You see, my ex-husband never finished college and here his wife was working on her second degree. I am not bragging. I know they had to question it. My family did. Needless to say, several days went past and I was still excited. I now believe that this bothered my husband because he was not the reason for my excitement. As a matter of fact, I was finding new ways to find happiness which was apart from him, and he will never admit this to anyone, but he did not like it. We would have a discussion several days later after me getting the letter, which would let him and me know a lot. You see, he started the talk back up about not being happy, and asking how I would feel if we got divorced.

He ultimately gave me an ultimatum which was that he would leave me if I decided to move forward in pursuing my graduate degree. It hurt, but I told him that I would help him pack and that no matter if he stayed or left, my life would go on and I would complete the program. He was extremely surprised by my response because he had hoped that it would be different. Needless to say, he did not leave; he actually ended up enrolling back into college to take a class.

Days later, he would share the news about him going back to school in a phone conversation with his family, and I would share my feelings with some of my family about making plans to leave him. There was nothing else to hide anymore. I was excited for his decision, but I recognized that I was married to someone that was not interested in me living my best life. I had come to know and understand that he would never genuinely be happy for anything that I would undertake. He would go through the motions, but it would be just that.

I know that you have had times where you have felt at your wits end. You may be there now, and want to throw in the towel. I completely understand.

We would continue to co-exist in the marriage for several more months until...

We had our final fight. It was a warm and sunny summer day. I ran into an old friend. She was my play niece and I will add, the cousin of my first love. I had known her since she was two years old. We had stopped talking because of my husband, who was my fiancé' at the time. She wanted to get together and catch up. I went home and talked to my husband and asked his permission. He was not particularly thrilled because of the connection, but he gave me permission. Several days later, she and I had lunch. I came home happy and feeling good. I had missed her. Not only that, I had not been this happy in such a long time, and I felt true joy.

My husband noticed and did not like it. He asked how things went and I told him. He told me that he had changed his mind and that I was no longer allowed to see her. I felt fire inside. I told him that I should never have had to ask his permission in the first place, but that I did and I reminded him that he gave it. He did not like the fact that I was happy again, and that the reason was outside of him. I told him that I would not tell her that we could not hang out, and all hell broke loose.

He was furious only took it a bit further this time. He had shared with me that he could not stand the sight of me, nor sleeping with me and many other things. I was not being obedient and on and on. I cried but pulled myself together because I realized that his intention was to hurt me, so that I would do what he wanted me to, which was his usual pattern. I also realized that there was no going back, and that we were over. He could not take back the things that he said, and I could not act as though I never heard them.

I asked him to leave, which was shocking to him. He asked when he could come back, and my internal dialogue yelled, "NEVER", but the words that came out of my mouth were "I do not know". He asked me if I wanted a divorce, and I said yes. Again, he seemed shocked. He knew that I meant it.

He fell into his pattern of wanting to talk, and doing everything he could to fix it. He apologized for what he said, but we both knew that he could not take anything back. I felt rage, hurt, and like my life was slowing unraveling before my very eyes. It was like a bad picture in a movie.

At least that is what it felt like. He left for a few days, and then he came back, and I told our daughter that we were getting a divorce. He went and stayed with his mother. My heart was breaking and being healed all at the same time because the lie was over but my journey was really just beginning.

Maybe your marriage is intact, but your issue is with your job. Perhaps you selected a specific career path, and believed that you would work your way up the corporate ladder, and spend the rest of your life working for that company only to lose your job, or quit.

Maybe you are like a friend of mine who had worked for a company for years, received her promotion at the corporate location only to find out that she hated her new job. Maybe you have always wanted to start your own business, write a book, or take a dream vacation but for some reason, you never did so.

If you have finished reading my story, you will see that I was clearly at a disadvantage. The plan that I had for my life had not worked out, and my marriage was over. I had made the decision to become a single mother, and had seemingly fell right into place where society would label me as a statistic, and put me in a "box" so to speak, or so they thought.

Let me tell you about the **advantage of disadvantage**. The advantage is that I found the courage to walk away from a relationship that did not serve me, and I found my voice. I also found peace, happiness and joy as well.

The advantage was I discovered my self-worth, and passion for living again. The advantage was I discovered that I could make it as a single mother. I realized that my divorce did not have to define me. It was an experience that would not destroy my future.

My destiny was not determined by it, and it had no power over me unless I allowed it.

The advantage is that I could share my story with so many people, and hope that they could see themselves somehow in my experience and be inspired to change. Let me share with you how I made it.

The Road To Discovery and Recovery

My road to discovery and recovery took time. I had to work through the pain, disappointment, shame, rage and anger. I felt shame because I failed to honor myself by staying in a marriage when I knew the season was over.

I felt disappointment because somehow I believed that I personally had failed, and that my daughter would someday resent me for leaving her father instead of staying and making it work. I felt anger and rage toward my husband and others, for unmet needs and less than ideal and unrealistic expectations. I had to feel it all.

I had to take time to get clear.

I had to pause and begin to get clear about what I wanted for myself, my family and my overall well-being. I began practicing meditation again every day for at least 30 minutes. Doing this helped to calm my mind, get quiet and feel more connected to God. I also journaled my feelings. Writing is very cathartic.

It allowed me a means of expressing my thoughts, feelings and emotions in a way that was safe for me. In this process, I had to begin to look within and ask myself some very deep and thought provoking questions. I needed to understand how I ended up in this situation.

I had betrayed myself by compromising my values and beliefs by living a lie, and remaining in a bad marriage, and I was angry, hurt, emotionally bankrupt and broken. I also had to look for the lessons that I needed to learn from my experience. I started a separate journal for my expressions of gratitude. I began to be grateful for the little things, such as time with my daughter, peaceful days and nights, and gratitude for new beginnings.

I also worked with a Christian counselor as well. This proved extremely useful as I attempted to understand certain patterns that I had created, and I learned new ways to break those patterns. It was important for me to understand the role that I played in this as well.

I failed to specifically ask my husband for what I needed early. I was trying to be the good wife instead of recognizing that my needs were just as important as anyone else's. I also acknowledged that there was a part of me that did not feel worthy of love in the first place.

This became obvious to me over time as I continued to search for truth. I chose the person that I married because of the way that he made me feel in the beginning, and when he stopped showing affection and doing the things that were important to me, I no longer felt loved. I am sure that you can relate. This was not the outcome that I would have chosen, and yet I experienced it.

My truth, was realizing that there were signs in the beginning that I ignored. My intuition, I ignored as well as I made excuses for things. There was a sinking feeling in my gut, which I realized that I should have paid closer attention to.

Pay attention to the signs.

If you ever find yourself feeling uneasy about an opportunity, or experience that you are having with someone, do not ignore this. Nobody knows you better than you do.

If you lack self-confidence, make sure that you have a support system in place to help you dig deep within to discover the issue, so that you can choose wisely.

I would like you to stop right now and think of a situation or life experience that occurred in your past where you had to make an important decision about something and you questioned the outcome. Maybe you are experiencing this now. Briefly describe the situation?

_____

_____

_____

_____

Write down at least 3 or 4 gut feelings, or questions that you asked yourself as you thought about this decision.

1. _____

2. _____

3. _____

4. _____

Write out what the outcome of the decision was that you made.

_____

_____

_____

_____

Finally, I want you to think of and identify any lessons learned as you thought through the process. Write them down.

1. _____

2. _____

3. _____

4. _____

"A man's mind may be likened to a garden, which may be intelligently cultivated or allowed to run wild; but whether cultivated or neglected, it must, and will, bring forth. If no useful seeds are put into it, then an abundance of useless weed seeds will fall therein, and will continue to produce their kind."

James Allen

Pay Attention to your thoughts and self-talk.

As I shared before, I read positive books by Joyce Meyer and Iyanla Vanzant. Doing this really helped me as I worked through some of the unhealthy negative self-talk that I did which had become an unconscious pattern that I had developed over the years. For every time I had a negative thought, I would open Joyce Meyer's Battlefield of the Mind book and start reading.

I also said positive affirmations to myself and out loud. For every negative thought I had, I would contradict it by speaking positive comments about myself and others until it felt normal. I also began to celebrate again the things that I loved about myself, my life and began doing daily practices of expressing gratitude for things, people and situations.

Understand that no experience is wasted.

This experience proved to be very key to me because I learned so much about myself along the way. When I first began sorting through and working through all of my feelings and emotions, it was so overwhelming. I had to realize that my marriage and the failure of it was necessary for my own personal growth and development. I learned lessons on love – for myself, my husband and my daughter. Having my daughter opened up my heart to be able to love in a way that I never knew. She has taught me how to receive love as well.

I also learned that you can show someone love by releasing them, and praying that they find happiness and love, and I learned that there is no better gift that I could give to myself than self-respect, self-love, and truth. I was worthy of it then and I am worthy of it now. I have also learned that I need to forgive myself for choices that I made as well.

It took time, close to five years, and much healing, but my ex-husband and I have been able to work together to raise our daughter. I am able to express sincere gratitude for the tremendous help that he and his wonderful wife have given. We have worked together to accommodate schedules, and have consistently remained flexible for events with family. This has been a joint effort. It was not easy in the beginning but we had the common goal of our daughter being raised healthy, happy and whole. In the beginning, I communicated with his wife because she and I could work together. When my daughter and I were able to communicate without hurt, the healing really began. He forgave me for divorcing him, and I forgave him for failing to show up in the way that I needed him to. There were some things that we agreed to disagree upon and moved forward.

Beloved, it does not matter what your life has looked like. Your past does not determine your future. You absolutely positively can begin again. You can overcome any situation or setback, and you can comeback stronger, healthier, and more powerful than you have ever been but you must begin by taking steps to change the direction of your life. You can begin doing this by changing the way that you view your situation, refocusing your thoughts on your goals, and taking the necessary action steps which will move you closer to living your best life.

I knew that I had a greater purpose, and you do to. Beloved, begin to walk in your greatness. God did not bring you here as a mistake. There is value in each and every experience that you have had up until now, and nothing you have done has been wasted. The experiences have been and can be the building blocks for you to discover your passion.

Are you ready to create a new vision for your life? Do you have a dream of beginning a new career, or starting a new business or project? Maybe you desire to write a book, go back to school to complete a degree, or want to rebrand yourself. Well guess what? You can do any of those things, and here is how. I can help you unlock the door to the next chapter of your life by working with you to identify self-sabotaging and self-defeating thought patterns and behaviors that have been holding you back. I will work with you to set goals, and show you how to take actionable steps as we work together to create the vision of living your best life.

About Monique Tucker

Monique Royal Tucker was born in Boulder, Colorado, but has spent over twenty years in St. Louis, Missouri, where she currently resides. She attended the University of Missouri-St. Louis where she pursued a degree in Social Work. Monique received her Bachelor of Social Work Degree in 1998. In 2003, she decided to pursue a graduate degree and so she enrolled in an accelerated MBA program at Lindenwood University. She completed the program, and received her Master's in Business Administration in 2005.

Monique is a phenomenal woman with a God-given calling to inspire, empower and motivate people to live their best lives. She is a proud member of Toastmasters International, a future author, and public speaker. It is her heart's desire to become a motivational speaker and life coach, traveling the country and speaking to people, delivering her powerful message and helping them to realize and take steps that can change their lives. She has an entrepreneurial spirit as well, and will one day start her own business. In her spare time, she loves reading, spending time with her daughter, family and friends. For any questions and other information, you can email her at **moniquect74@gmail.com.**

Staring Stuttering in the Face

By Cicone Prince

Adolescence can be a trying time for most children. From growth spurts to hormones and even having your voice changing it can be a difficult time of transition. Add a speech impediment and you have a recipe for disaster. And that was my story. An eleven-year-old middle school boy having to report to speech therapy class was bad enough, but having to report to social studies class first and have my classmates ridicule me only added insult to injury. You see, stuttering had been a problem for me from my early childhood and had only gotten worse the older I got.

Have you ever had a problem that got progressively worse as time has gone by? And you find yourself at a loss as to how to solve it? I want to offer you three tips for help you confront any problem that you are facing and resolve it.

1. Acknowledge the Problem

Dr. Phil said that you can't fix what you won't acknowledge and my grandmother said it like this, "you can't fix what you won't face". Problems are a part of life. That reminds me of a story of a neighborhood boy who had just won a foot race with one of his friends and he was challenged by another boy who noticed that his shoe had come a loose.

You know the kind that flaps when you walk? But he was too full of pride to fix it but he didn't want to forfeit the race. He accepted the challenge without acknowledging that his shoe was loose. Needless to say he ran the race, tripped, fell, busted his lip, scraped his knee and lost the race. All of that happened because he wouldn't acknowledge his problems.

I had to acknowledge that I had a stuttering problem. I had to admit that I had a problem getting my words out. I had to own up to the fact that I had a hard time communicating.

Can you think of any problems that you have had that you have been unwilling to admit? Maybe a problem at work with a co-worker? Maybe a problem with a child or family member? Maybe you have had a problem with your health?

None of those problems will ever be resolved if you try to ignore them. Regardless of what the problem is you won't fix it if you don't face it.

Getting Unstuck

We've all been stuck at different points in our lives, whether we were stuck in line, stuck in traffic and some of us have been stuck in a bad relationship. We've even been stuck in a dead end job. My stuttering had me stuck. Stuck inside my head and not able to get my words out. But the thing about being stuck is that you don't have to stay there. And I want to offer you three strategies on how to stop stuttering at life that will help you get unstuck.

> A. Realize that you haven't reached your destination.

If you were flying to Hawaii and you had to stop in L.A. and you were stuck in the airport there, you would know that you haven't made it to your destination. Because L.A. was not your destination, Hawaii was. Now if you were in Hawaii - where you wanted to be – you wouldn't say I'm stuck in Hawaii. The only reason you would say that is because Hawaii wasn't your final destination.

Realize that you haven't made it to your destination. Saying one or two words is not a complete sentence. You have to get all the information out.

B. Recognize that it's only temporary.

Take a deep breath and breathe. Not only when you speak but in life, as well. Sometimes we have to just step back and regroup in order to move forward. We have to realize that it's not going to last forever, it's only temporary. You know, I remember seeing this magazine that had this advertisement on the back that was really interesting because it had a bunch of traffic lights and every light as far as you could see was green.

I thought to myself, "If I'm driving in a car on the street with all these green lights, I know sooner or later I'm going to have to stop." Because they're not going to be green by the time I get there. There is no way for you to keep going without having to stop. So being stuck is only temporary. Stuttering was only temporary and realizing that made it easier for me to look forward to the day that it was not going to detonate my life.

C. Remember why you started in the first place.

I started speech therapy in order to change the outcome of my life. To remember your destination; to remember why you are going and not to stay where you are. Somebody once said that a rut is a grave with the ends kicked out. So why stay there?

Remember why you started. Remember why you started on this journey, why you're started chasing your goals, why you started in this relationship. You have to remember. Don't just stay stuck at a point that is temporary, don't just get stuck at a point that's not your destination. But remember why you started.

2. Address the Problem

"It's better to do something imperfectly, than to do nothing flawlessly."
Robert Shula

The quickest way for us to delay getting to our goals is for us is to not address the issues. You may have an issue on your job, with your employees, you may have issues at home with your children. In my case I had to address my stuttering problem. I had to come to a place where, not only did I stop ignore my stuttering but I had to address it head on. It had become something that was not welcome anymore. What problems have you had that you didn't know what to do, but you knew something needed to be done?

I remember the second house that my wife and I moved in to. The laundry room was 20 feet away from the house in the back yard. Needless to say this was not the ideal condition to wash clothes when it was cold, raining, foggy or late. In other words it was a problem. I took it upon myself to address this problem head on. I went and purchased all of the parts that I thought I needed and set a day and time to get to work. Early one Saturday morning I shut off the water and proceeded to do my best handyman impersonation. I pulled pipes, glued pipes, clamped pipes and checked pipes.

I thought I had done everything I needed to do to setup a washer and dryer inside. After all the work was done I trotted outside to the water vale and proceeded to turn the water on. Thinking that I had succeed at my mission I slowly walked back to the house with my chest stuck out. My wife came to the door franticly yelling turn it off! Turn it off! Water's going everywhere! I was willing to address the problem but my solution was not the right fix.

Even with my stuttering, not talking or being shy was not going to correct my speech impediment. I had to address it head on. I signed up for a speech therapy class in my middle school in order to address my problem.

3. Attack the Problem

Even after addressing my problem there still wasn't a solution. I couldn't just go through the material, I had to let the material go through me. After I learned the techniques needed to help me with my speech problem I then had to relentlessly use them in order to better myself. In other words, I had to attack the problem.

Over and over again, I had to practice and speak as much and as often as I could. I began by doing little parts in Church plays and saying Easter speeches. I would opt to run meetings for small groups and I began talking more that way. I had to keep hammering if I was going to overcome this problem.

It's like a baby learning to walk. We've all seen babies learning how to walk and every now and then, they'll fall. And we'll come and help them get up and dust themselves off and get going again. Well my question to you is, have you ever had anything in your life that has caused you to fall?

Maybe it was a relationship. Maybe it was a situation on your job. Maybe it was even with your finances. All of us, we have experience with some type of fall. My stuttering was a fall and that can be a problem. The thing is getting up from it. Don't just stay there; don't just lay there, but get up.

You know you can generally tell how bad a fall is by how long someone stays down. Some people have been down for a long time. They've been down for years. They've had their heart broken and don't want to get up. Stuttering kept me from talking and expressing myself. I had fallen and I didn't want to get up. But I want to encourage you to get up and get going. Get back in the race.

You know that reminds me of a story of this guy who was running a race and they were running around the track. In the very first turn he fell. All the other runners kept going but he fell and tumbled. Everybody said, "Oh, Ooooh! That was such a bad fall!"

But, he got up and he kept going! He kept running the race. Well, about half the way through he fell again and this time he fell even harder. This time he had bruises and he was bleeding. But he got up and he kept running.

Are you going to get up from your fall? Are you going to continue going on in the directions that you planned and esteemed to go? Are you still looking at that goal? I had to do that with my speech therapy. I had to keep showing up!

The guy kept running the race and by this time everyone else finished but he wanted to make sure that he crossed the finish line.

He ran a little further and he fell again, and by this time people were like, "Why don't you stop?", "Why don't you just give up?", "Why don't you just walk off the track?"

But no, he wanted to finish the race. So guess what?... He got up again, and he kept running... Until he crossed the finish line and by the time he finished everybody was standing on their feet cheering because what he did, he embodied that "Never Give Up!" that, "Never Quit" Spirit!

Just because you've fallen, have a problem or a setback, just because you've had a hard turn doesn't mean that you have to stop and give up. We all have to learn how to Get Up From a Fall!

And I have done just that by facing my Stuttering problem and you can do the same! I don't care what the problem is you have to:

1. Acknowledge the Problem

2. Address the Problem

3. Attack the Problem

By doing so you can Stare Stuttering (or your Problem) in the Face and Win!

About Cicone Prince

Mr. Prince is a highly sought after Motivational Speaker, a renowned Author, and Personal Development Strategist that helps people take an objective look at themselves. He is the President and CEO of CiconePrince.com and their slogan is "Introducing You to Yourself."™

He is also the former President and CEO of 3D Solution Providers, LLC. This business experience has served as a classroom for developing content for his motivational speaking, authoring and personal development.

With an Associate's Degree in Electronics and a Bachelor's Degree in Electronic Engineering, Mr. Prince has used his love of learning to continue educating himself. He then passes on those lessons via engaging stories and illustration during his motivational speeches.

Mr. Prince latest book, **"Are You Climbing The Wrong Mountain? Finding Your True Purpose"** explores the possibility that you are not living up to your full potential on your current career path. A copy of it can be purchased from Amazon.com. His first book, **"Are You Smart Enough To Play Dumb"** is available as a free download from his website www.ciconeprince.com.

Mr. Prince is married to Yolanda Prince and they have 5 children, Marcellus, Christin, Jessica, Taylor and Jonathan.

cicone@ciconeprince.com

The Quiet Storm

By Dr. Nekeshia C. Doctor

OPENING: The Silence Struggle

As the firstborn daughter of a 15-year old teenage girl, I was raised in a single-parent home for the first 10 years of my life with loving support from my teen mother and family. Considering the fact that my maternal grandmother passed away when my mother was three years old, she had a village of relatives and friends to help my grandfather raise her and her siblings. As a result of the village, my mother had similar support while raising me and my sister, whom my mother gave birth to two years later after me.

Although I received and felt love from my mother and family growing up, when I was of age to understand, I often felt as though I was a mistake and burden because I was the by-product of a 15-year old teenager who was still a child herself. Despite any odds, my mother took pride in raising me and my sister. She never treated us differently or demonstrated any favoritism. If my mother ever noticed that others treated us differently, she would address it. There were occasions where relatives or family friends would want to take either of us home with them for a weekend and my mother would immediately say, you can't take one without the other child.

Even though my mother did not raise us differently, I discerned a difference from others as I grew older. I took notice of how relatives, friends, and even strangers would treat my sister and I differently. My sister has the golden-brown skin tone, plump cute cheeks with dimples, and nice thick legs that people always complimented in such a jovial way.

They would make comments such as "She is adorable. She is so pretty with those cute, little dimples." However, I have a pecan, dark-brown skin tone, long structured facial features, and beautiful coarse hair, but my compliments never matched those given to my sister. Others would notice me and simply say, "You look just like your mother." As a child, it would make me smile to hear that I resembled my beautiful mother. Yet, it still felt different compared to how people responded to my baby sister.

Twenty-one years later, I still clearly remember a very offensive comment that a classmate of mine made to me. One day after band practice while waiting on my sister to be dismissed from chorus rehearsal, he asked me why was I still at the school. I responded and told him that I was waiting on my sister. Shortly thereafter, my sisters walked up and my classmate said, "This is your sister! Well, what happened to you?"

I felt so humiliated by such a rude comment made right in front of my sister. He would always find something sarcastic or offensive to say to me; I suppose because I was reserved and quiet, never bothering anyone. Although I am the oldest daughter and always felt as though it was my duty to protect my sister and not allow her to see my insecurities, but strength, I wrestled with my own internal and external beauty.

Mountain out of a Molehill

When I was 10 years old, my mother married my amazing stepfather who accepted my sister and I as if we were his own biological daughters. My sister and I quickly gave him the name of "Pops" and he's been just that for us for the past twenty plus years. Regardless of my parent's love and protection, the mental and emotional battle that I had within me grew from a molehill to a mountain. I did not feel attractive because I felt as though others did not find me beautiful or appealing. I always felt as though I had to work at being beautiful on the outside, unlike my sister, family members, and some of my peers who were naturally beautiful, if not "drop-dead" gorgeous to me.

Additionally, I felt as if I had to always work twice as hard academically while in grade school than my sister. My sister was the academic scholar who was always recognized for her academic ability by way of the A/B Honor Roll, National Honor Society, Black Junior Achievers, etc. So, in my eyes, my sister had the beauty and the brains.

As a teenager, I was shy, quiet, and much of an introvert. I was also a bit withdrawn from others unless I felt some form of connection and could trust someone. I had difficulty accepting compliments from peers and adults because I was unsure if they were genuine. I had grown accustomed to my sister receiving all of the compliments. So, when someone did recognize me, I did not know how to accept it. I always replied in such a way that I did not receive it.

For example, if someone told me that my hair was beautiful and nice. I would say something such as "Oh, I need to get it done again or I need a relaxer" instead of simply saying thank you. I had friendships that I valued, but would only allow friends to get so close to me. This was my way of protecting my heart and shielding my feelings of unwanted hurt and rejection.

On March 8, 1992, I accepted Jesus Christ as Lord and Savior of my life at the age of 15 because I wanted to rid this battle within my mind. I came to understand that He was my help in the time of trouble and would hide me in His secret place. Being that He is not a physical being, I trusted Him to not hurt me. I asked God to change my heart and do something new in me.

As a young lady in my early 20's, I still recall struggling with identifying my self-worth and purpose in life. I felt worthless as though I had no relevance on this earth. I found myself trying to compensate for my own insecurities by making others happy and keeping them laughing. I have always enjoyed serving and helping others, which allowed me to take my mind off of how I felt about myself. Inspiring others, no matter the age, came natural for me, but I rarely could empower myself and discover my purpose in life and thrive.

All the while thinking that I did not matter in this world and my physical features did not exemplify beauty, God revealed something to me through my sister. During our early adulthood, my sister and I were simply having a conversation and out of nowhere she said to me, "I would give the world to have a long, structured face like yours." I immediately asked her why.

She replied, "Because I think that it's very beautiful and that is what they look for in the modeling industry as well." My sister's compliment really made me feel relevant and special because she was the one that everyone paid attention to. And while others were giving her attention, she was watching me.

Rebooted and Renewed...Relevant Me

The Awakening

One day, after receiving a thoughtful gift from my mother, I had an awakening and it changed my life. It changed my life because my way of thinking shifted. The gift my mother gave me was a picture of a lion looking at itself in the mirror with a quote that stated, "YOU ARE YOUR ONLY LIMITATION."

As a way to help transform my thinking, I would keep this picture on my desk in my classroom as a teacher as well as on my desk in my office as a school administrator.

I chose to do this to not only inspire me daily, but my students, parents, teachers, and anyone who noticed it on my desk. I wanted to empower them to take the limits off of themselves and aim high. It was my desire to encourage others to press pass the self-doubt, fear, insecurities and get rid of the "head trash" that was suffocating their mind.

The quote on the picture became one of my first personal affirmations that I declared out of my mouth everyday as a reminder to keep going no matter what and that if I didn't stop, I've defeated myself. I would have no one to blame or give credit to negative energy, but ME.

Over time, I began to realize that the POWER was inside of me all along! **Simon T. Bailey** said it well, *"Everything you need is already inside of you. Stop looking outside for what exists inside."*

I understood that I have the POWER to speak or think life over death by the words I choose to speak out of my mouth and the thoughts I choose to give energy to and take up space in my mind. The light turned on for me in my head. We have the power to give control to that which we want to. I recognized that I did not need the approval of others to feel beautiful internally and externally. All that I needed to do was activate my own power.

The Prescribed Process

We can only progress in live as far as we allow ourselves to. I believe that our level of prosperity and success in life is predicated by each of us individually and the limits we place on our lives. I overcame my social inhibitions by declaring daily affirmations over my life such as ***"I AM a designer's original. I AM beautiful and matter in this world. I AM relevant"***

Then, I created a daily regimen to continue self-empowerment. Please understand that one has to want it; want it greater and I wanted it bad. I was ready to transform from "stuck in a rut" to "ALIVE and THRIVING." My daily regimen is what I call the "P.O.W.E.R." prescription. My daily dosage empowers me to:

P- Practice loving myself daily;

O- Open my eyes & ears to who God created me to be.

W- Walk it out; stay the course until I see results, even when the going gets tough and it hurts.

E- Express myself to me and others through effective communication; Elevate my thinking and how I see myself;

R- Realize that there is greatness inside of me and look for opportunities to grow

The Outcome

Despite the course of my struggles and battling with my inner enemy, I still experienced some triumph. It was upon earning my Doctorate degree in Education that I was able to see that my teenage mother's journey and choice to keep and raise me was not a mistake. I understand that there are NO illegitimate children, only illegitimate parents. The only mistake made was that the people that crossed paths with me on my journey to the breakthrough, missed a pivotal opportunity to get to genuinely know me for who I was becoming and the power that lay within me.

Society would say that I beat the odds. However, it is important to know that you don't have to beat the odds, the odds have to beat you. In the end, you are the ultimate decision maker and nothing else matters. So, the odds didn't have to beat me because I was the decision maker!

Today, as a by-product of a teenage mother, my passion, life, and work as an educator, mentor, author, and Founder/Executive Director of a 501(c)3 nonprofit organization, are all about opening new windows of possibility for girls and women who have been challenged by their staggered mindsets and choices and seeking a path to make the most of their lives. Today, I am able to say that I am FREE of mental and emotional bondage. I have the power aligned with a courageous mind and spirit to take on the world and never look back, but use my past struggles as a stepping stone to go higher.

About Dr. Nekeshia C. Doctor

Dr. Nekeshia C. Doctor is a passionate educator of 15 years who is zealous about coaching, mentoring, and supporting parents, youth, and educators to excel at their highest potential and obtain unlimited possibilities. She empowers youth from various walks of life to recognize who they are; embrace who they were divinely created to be; love themselves first, and stand in their own brilliance.

She is CEO of JALIA Consulting, Inc. Her ability to empower others and build a positive culture within any household or organization speaks for itself. She is also Founder/Executive Director of The BW Project, Inc., a 501(c)3 nonprofit organization that focuses on self-empowerment, self-confidence, self-sufficiency, leadership, and respect tailored to girls between the ages of 8-18 years old. Dr. Doctor is an active member of Delta Sigma Theta Sorority, Inc.

Dr. Doctor believes that life is about conquering our social inhibitions and extending a hand to help and bless others who may share those same fears.

As you discover your brilliance, EMBRACE it, OWN it, and STAND in it with no apologies.

drnlcd@gmail.com

A Journey Called Life

By Jennifer Tuley

Welcome and thank you for joining me on this journey called life! My name is Jennifer Tuley and my business is the Breakthrough Success Academy. What I do is work with individuals to look beyond their current circumstances, break through any limiting beliefs, and attain the success they desire in life or business. Through my research, work, and study, I have come to realize that the struggles that I faced in my early life were much like the struggles that so many young girls and women deal with.

Because of that, I have dedicated my life and my work to helping individuals see their greater worth, recognize and foster their skills and talents, and reinvent themselves to be whatever they desire to be. For that, I have been recognized as the Image Reinvention Expert, helping women and girls of all ages reinvent themselves to be whatever they desire.

I grew up in rural mid-west Michigan in a loving, supportive, middle- class family. My mother stayed home with my sister and me while my father was worked as Chief Psychologist for a state-run regional mental health facility. By anyone's view, I had a typical childhood and upbringing. I was an average student and participated in track, ran competitive cross-country, of which we were state champions several years, and I was part of several choir groups. After graduating high school, I went off to college like all of my friends — because that's what I thought I was supposed to do; it's what all my friends were doing. But very quickly, I realized that I just didn't feel like I belonged there.

It was like everyone around me held this secret as to what they were going to do with their lives, like they had received some magic letter giving them their destiny, and I had somehow missed out on that. I really didn't have any idea what I wanted to do with my life, and instead of taking advantage of all the opportunities that college offered to find those things out, I let my fear and uncertainty take over.

I let my insecurities take hold, and became paralyzed by that fear rather than using it to explore all the opportunities available to me. I became more and more disinterested and left after a year and a half.

Feeling like a complete failure, I came home. What was I supposed to do with my life now? All my friends were still in college, and here I was at home.

Where was I going, what was I going to do? Continuing to search for my purpose in life, I decided maybe a change of scenery would help me get that clarity I was searching for. I moved to Indiana with my sister to "get a fresh start." I still struggled with where I fit in. What was my place in this life? What was I meant to do or be or have? And why did it seem like I was the only one who felt that way?

I took a position with Starbucks Coffee Company to pay the bills and fill up my time. Seemed like a good idea; I could drink coffee and talk to people all day! Very quickly I found my niche and rose up through the ranks. I really enjoyed the work and my efforts did not go unnoticed.

Within a year, I was General Manager of several stores and was beginning to see a career path for myself. It wasn't an area that I had ever considered, but I was learning that it wasn't so scary to try new things. It was during this period of discovery and growth that I met my husband. We fell in love and shortly after got married. It was through his encouragement that

I realized that while I really liked what I was doing, I was not fulfilled. While the recognition was nice, there was still a need deep within me that was not being met. With his support, I left Starbucks and returned to school. I completed my degree in surgical technology and finally felt like I was working for a purpose! I loved the process of the work, the limitless amount of knowledge I could gain, and the excitement that each new day brought. But, again, I found myself wanting more.

Why was I not being fulfilled in each of these roles I was taking on? What was I searching for? It was during this period of searching for something more, that I met some individuals who fueled my desire to become more and push myself to limits that I didn't even know I could go to. They introduced me to skills, knowledge, and a profession that I didn't even know existed.

They introduced to me all those things I had still been wanting out of my career. But most importantly, they introduced me to a different way of thinking, not only about our profession, but about myself. They taught me that whatever I wanted to make happen in my life could be by simply believing in it.

This opened up a whole new world for me, but it also brought up so many feelings and thoughts that I had pushed away for most of my life. I had a very negative self-image as a young girl. There were times I was picked on and teased, made fun of and excluded from groups or activities.

This set me up for a mindset that included a lifetime of low self-confidence and questioning of my self-worth. I now believe that this is one of the reasons I struggled when I initially went off to college. This, along with several other circumstances in my life, only strengthened the feelings of negativity and self-doubt that I was having.

These new colleagues helped me to change how I viewed myself, my worth, and my contributions to the world. I learned that while I was the only one who had the power to change how I felt about myself, the great news was that I WAS the one who had the power about how I felt about myself. I also learned that if I didn't believe in myself, how could I ever expect anyone else to believe in me?

Eleanor Roosevelt said, "No one can ever make you feel inferior without your consent." But what if you are the one making yourself feel inferior? What if you are the one giving the consent to allow your own demise?

Through extensive self-discovery, I have learned that it is possible to change your life simply by changing how you think, feel, and talk about yourself. I have helped countless others learn how to attain the levels of success they desire in their life through these small inner changes, as it is only when we do the work inside that our life on the outside changes. Through my work, I came to realize that who I am and whatever I am, that It IS ENOUGH!

I learned that the contributions that I make to the world are significant and worthy and beneficial. I can help you realize that the way you think about yourself, talk about/to yourself and the actions that you carry out based on how you think and talk about yourself have the power to change your life! YOU hold the power to change anything about your life and it all begins with what you think about yourself.

How you do anything is how you do everything. If you want to be excellent in your work, you cannot be mediocre in your self-worth. You must live your life with a level of congruency through all dimensions, and it must begin with looking in the mirror.

I have faced struggles and difficulties in my life which have helped me to realize that it is up to me to be my own advocate, to be my own biggest cheerleader, and that no one can ever love me more than I love myself. Throughout these chapters, I will help you to see how changing how you think about yourself will be the catalyst for making any other changes in your life.

Change One Thing will help you to see that by simply changing how you think about yourself can change your entire life, and by doing this, you can make any other change in your life that you desire.

> ***"Your self-worth has nothing to do with your craft or calling, and everything to do with how you treat yourself."***
>
> ***Kris Carr***

Are you living the life you have always dreamed of?

Are you interested and open to the limitless possibilities for your life?

Have you ever experienced some level of self-doubt in your life? Maybe about a project you were working on. Or you questioned a decision that you had made or a decision that you didn't make. Or perhaps you have wondered about what the next step in your life was going to be. Well, I'm here to tell you something, I know how you feel.

One of the reasons that I wanted to write this and why I am so passionate about this subject is that I know exactly how you feel. I've been there, and I know what that self-doubt feels like. I found myself at a point in my life where the image that I had of myself didn't match the image that I wanted to project to the world. I found that the way that I thought of myself and the way that I talked to myself were one way, but when I thought about what I was actually saying, well, I would never allow anyone else to say those things to me, or anyone I cared about.

So why was I allowing myself to talk to myself that way? In fact, if anyone else had ever tried to talk to me the way that I talked to myself, I would have knocked them out! You see, I **was** my worst critic. I was my own biggest enemy. And I now truly believe that the only reason I didn't accomplish the things that I set out to do was because I didn't believe that I could do it. I didn't believe in myself or believe that I was worthy of deserving of the good in my life.

So I set out on a mission of self-discovery. I wanted to figure out why was it that the image I had of myself that I did. I wanted to know why the image that I had didn't match the image that I wanted to project to the world. One of the most enlightening revelations of my research was that so many people I've talked to have had similar experiences. So now I HAD to figure out why we feel this way!

I started doing some research to try and figure out why it was that so many of us think so poorly of ourselves and end up being our own worst critics? And what I found was startling. I will share this information with you over the following pages to allow you to see for yourself, just what our young girls and women deal with. We must begin the process of changing our self-image and through awareness and insight, we can all reinvent ourselves.

I read a statistic from Self magazine that stopped me in my tracks. They interviewed a group of girls between the ages of 10 and 14, and what they found out was astonishing to me. Statistically, 82 percent of these girls did not like themselves. They didn't like who they were as a person, or how they looked, or how others perceived them. That's right! That means that only 18 girls out of 100 actually liked who they were as a person!

Shocking! What does that say about the image and the impression that we project onto the young girls around us?

What does it say about the young girls who have a negative self-image, who grow up to be young women and the women of our workforce and society today? How do they feel about themselves? What decisions do they make about their lives given this image of themselves that they have?

In her article, "Media, Hormones, Peer Pressure Do A Number On Girls' Confidence", from The News-Gazette, July 31, 2006, Carol McGraw states that a girls' self-esteem peaks when she is only nine years old! With that being said, every impression, idea, and thought that girls younger than this age have, THIS forms the foundation for their self-images **for the rest of their lives!**

I recently had the opportunity to attend a women's empowerment conference that was focused on helping women find all the amazing gifts within ourselves and how to apply all those gifts to the different aspects of our lives. This was a multi-generational conference and even included a family of four generations of women, the youngest was only 14 years old. When this young girl was asked what she wanted to achieve out of this process, she stated that she just wanted more self-confidence so she wouldn't be teased so much at school.

This beautiful girl was being teased, made fun of, and bullied. And as I looked into the eyes of this vibrant girl, I realized that I felt like I was looking into my own eyes. Years ago, I WAS that girl. I was teased, made fun of, and told "no wonder kids didn't want to be friends with me".

I think the thing that made it so hurtful was that it was said by influential teachers at a young age. But also, as I sat there watching what seemed like a movie of my own life, at that moment, what I realized as I looked at this innocent soul was that I was no longer that girl.

While I could see the pain and torment in her eyes, and literally feel the torture she was enduring on a daily basis, I realized that I had made a conscious choice to no longer accept the label that had been given to me – the label that I then took as my scarlet letter and wore as my badge of shame.

As I stand back and look at that image of myself at that age, I realize that she is no longer me. She is no longer serving a purpose in my life. I have loved her and mourned the torment she had to endure, the labels that were placed on her, the decisions she made at different points in her life because of the things people had told her and the restrictions she put on her life because of that lack of self-confidence.

But *I* was no longer *her*. She did not define who I was now as a person. I made a conscious decision to not allow the image I had of myself to dictate who I was for the rest of my life.

- More than 90 percent of girls age 15 to 17 want to change at least one aspect of their physical appearance, with body weight being the highest ranked.

- Obese boys and girls have significantly lower self-esteem than their non-obese peers.

- Seven in ten girls believe that they are not good enough or do not measure up to their peers in some way, including their looks, performance in school, and in relationships.

So what we are finding is that based on how these young people feel about themselves, they are talking themselves out of working to their highest potential in school, missing out on daily activities due to how they feel about themselves, and getting into less than ideal relationships because they feel they do not deserve any better.

Ladies and gentlemen, these young people are our future! They are our children who are making poor decisions, our siblings and loved ones who are in relationships that are destructive and possibly even abusive. They are our sisters and mothers, our wives and our daughters. We MUST help them see themselves differently if we want to have any hope of helping them reach their ultimate goals in life.

Why do people get stuck living in the image they had of themselves at such an early age? Why do we settle for a life of ordinary, when we were meant to be extraordinary? Think about each of the following emotions. How has each emotion affected you in your life? Take a moment and work through this list.

- Fear
- Insecurity
- Uncertainty
- Regrets
- Regrets

- Uncertainty
- Insecurity
- Self-doubt
- Inadequacy

What can we do to break these habits, stop these behaviors, change our thinking, and discover the amazing power we have within ourselves? For me, it took getting a coach. I was not able to see how to stop the negative thinking and move forward with my goals in life. It took someone else pointing them out to me, forcing me to look deep inside myself and re-evaluate my thinking about everything, but most importantly, about how I felt about myself. You see, sometimes we can't see the whole picture because we are in the frame. It takes someone looking in from the outside, an impartial observer, to point out the habits, the behavior, or the actions, to allow us to really see what is going on in our lives.

What is a coach and why is it important to the growth process? The process of coaching involves addressing specific personal goals, projects, professional desires, personal life transitions, relationships, and obstacles. It is concerned with discovering what challenges the client may be facing that have hindered their progress in completion of life goals or achievement of the level of success one desires.

The coach and client work together to choose a course of action that is appropriate to the goals voiced by the client. So how do you know if you need a coach? Do you think Michael Jordan ever questioned whether he needed a coach? Do you think Muhammad Ali ever wondered if he really needed Angelo Dundee? Do you think that Tiger Woods could have ever risen to the level of success that he has without the assistance, guidance, and coaching of Hank Haney? I would argue no to each question. The best athletes in the world all have a coach. The highest ranking leaders of major corporations all have advisors.

The President of the United States of America has a cabinet that advises him of the happenings of the world and makes recommendations to him as to what they believe his actions should be. So my point is this ... all of the most successful people in the world have a coach, so why don't you? Don't YOU deserve to be the best? Don't you deserve a life of unparalleled success, of limitless possibilities, of joy and happiness on a level you've never dreamed possible? I believe you do! And it's time for you to believe that you do, too!

It's time for you to face the man in the mirror. It's time for you to ask HIM to make the change!

Michael Jackson truly said it best, I believe. If you want to make the world a better place, you have to take a look at yourself ... and then MAKE that change!

As with any major life change, it has to come from a deep desire within yourself. It won't be easy. It will take lots of hard work, dedication, and commitment. But it will be worth it. It's been said that not everything that is hard is worth it, but everything that is worth it WILL be hard.

It will be up to you to put in the work, to stay dedicated, and stay the course of the commitment. It will mean you have to make some tough decisions. You will have to ask yourself the following questions:

- Are there things in your life that are standing in the way of your success?
- Are there people that are hindering your progress by continually putting thoughts in to your head that are negative or dismissive?

You must make that conscious decision to only surround yourself with those who will bring you closer to your goals; those who support your vision and push you to work harder than you thought you had in you. But in the end, it's up to you.

Take some time to think through the following questions. Use the accompanying workbook to record your answers, thoughts, and goals.

1. What are some decisions you are going to have to make to take the next step in moving closer to your goals?

2. If you could change just one thing about yourself today that would make all your dreams come true, that would give you ultimate happiness, and would set you on a course for the greatest success in your life, what would that one thing be?

What if I told you that all of that could be yours with only one change? Well, it's possible. You see, what if that one change was the way you think about yourself?

- Do you believe you deserve it?
- Do you believe you are worth it?
- Are you smart enough?
- Are you kind or generous enough?
- Are you attractive enough?

Yes, yes, yes, yes, and YES!!!!

What if by changing the way you think about yourself, the way you talk about yourself, and the actions you manifest because of the way you think and talk about yourself, what if changing those simple little things could change the course of your destiny? Well, I'm here to tell you, that it worked for me, and I know it will work for you. You must begin by changing how you think about yourself. Like Michael Jackson said, "Its time to start with the Man in the Mirror."

"Walk the Walk. Talk the Talk".

So often we hear people say "if only you could walk in my shoes, you would know how difficult life is for me." But what if we could walk in someone else's shoes? What would we see? Would we live their lives differently, make different decisions than theirs? It's so easy to see the solutions to others' problems when we are looking from the outside. But how do we identify and find the solutions to the areas of concern in our own life? How do we step back, step out of the frame, and look at our lives from the outside in? By identifying one thing in your life that you want to change, this becomes a catalyst for all other changes you may want to make. But it all begins with stepping back and identifying what you want to change.

Take a few moments and identify a few areas of your life that you feel you are very successful or satisfied with. Write them down in your accompanying workbook.

What is it about these things that makes you feel successful or satisfied?

What habits, traits, or behaviors do you exhibit when engaged in these activities or areas?

Would you consider yourself "excellent" in these areas? What is it that makes you excellent?

Numerous studies have proven that how you do anything is how you do everything; therefore, excellence is a habit! If you want to make this initial change in your life, you will have to dedicate the same passion, time, and dedication hard work to the new habits and behavior as you do to the areas that you consider yourself to be excellent.

Undoubtedly, we are always drawn to the things we haven't done in our lives; the things we gave up on, didn't finish, or never started at all. This is what we term regret. We all have regrets in our lives. We have all done things that we wish we could change, take back, or somehow make different.

> *"Regret for the things we have done can be tempered with time, but it's regret for the things we have not done, that is inconsolable."*
>
> *Sydney J. Harris*

What have you not done in your life that you wish you would have, or could have, or think you should do? It is our duty to leave this life empty; to have given everything to every idea, project, and decision we are faced with. Doing anything but less is wasting the life we've been given. Through my work and research, I have developed a proven plan for changing those could've-should've-would've's into the steps to make that necessary change: **C-W-S**

C = Control. Take control over the things in your life that you can.

There are many things that we choose to do, but there are also a great number of things we can control, such as our attitude. What does your attitude say about how you view your life and the world around you? Are you positive, always thinking of how to move forward? Or do you tend to look at new ideas with skepticism, negativity, or disbelief? Take a mental inventory of your attitude for a day. What does it say about you? Your attitude directly affects your altitude. How high are you going to go with your current attitude?

You also can control who you hang around with. They say that you are the sum total of the six people you hang around with the most. What do the behaviors of your friends/acquaintances say about you? Are they living the life you want to be living? Are they working every day to move closer to their goals and dreams? Or are they dream-busters, taking advantage of every opportunity to kill your dreams and everyone else's who dares to have a dream or goal? Are there some relationships that you need to sever, some people that, to move to the next level in your life, you need to separate yourself from?

And finally, you have control over what you listen to and put into your mind. Are you taking time each day to fill your mind with positive, motivating, dream-building information? Are you talking to yourself in a positive, life-affirming way? Or are you the first to convince yourself that you can't do something? If you don't first believe it, how will anyone else ever believe you? As human beings, we are so focused on making sure that everyone else is happy, satisfied, and has have all their needs met. But what about our own needs? How can we be effective for anyone else, if our own needs are not being met? This must come from within.

We must take time every day to meet our own needs, to fill our own mind, to fill our own cup. Then and only then are we able to fill everyone else's cup from our overflow. Set aside time each day, preferably at the same time each day, to spend on you. Read positive material, listen to something inspiring, and recite positive affirmations to yourself. Remember, Control what you can!

S = Sacrifice. We must sacrifice what is comfortable for what is necessary.

When choosing to make any change in your life, it will be necessary to make some sacrifices. Sacrificing old habits, behaviors, and even relationships may be necessary. Oftentimes, one of the main reasons change does not last is because it is too easy to fall back into our old habits. We even tell ourselves, "Well, if it doesn't work out, I can always go back to ...." What if we took out the backup plan? What if we decided that going back to our old ways was not an option? It will take sacrifice to make that decision, to decide that comfortable is no longer an option. Comfortable does not get us to the goals and dreams we have. For any change to be lasting and effective, it is going to be uncomfortable. It MUST be. Again I tell you, not everything hard is worth it, but I guarantee you that everything worth it is GOING to be hard!

Remember, a caterpillar cannot become a butterfly by simply wishing that it was so. It must go through painful, dark, life-altering work to emerge as a butterfly. It must cut itself off from everything in the outside world – food, water, light, all of its comforts – for what? To become a beautiful butterfly. And only when it has completed all the necessary work, will it emerge; only when it is ready will the hard work reveal itself.

And so it is with you.

You must put in the hard work. It may require that you cut yourself off from some outside influences or distractions. It may require some pain and hardship. But when that work is done, you will emerge as a new person, leaving only the skeleton of your old life behind. Commit to the Sacrifice. It will be worth it!

W=The Will.

What does will have to do with change? Everything! Is it the drive, the determination, the strength? Yes! And you must develop each of these things if you want lasting change in your life. Werner von Braun was a German rocket scientist, aerospace engineer, and architect. He served as an advisor to NASA in the development and initial launch of the Saturn V and Apollo spacecraft, under the administration of President John F. Kennedy. While having a last-minute discussion regarding the safety and logistics of actually putting man into space, von Braun said that there was a very easy answer to all their questions.

An answer that was as simple as five words: "The will to do it." Before this time, the idea of putting anything into space, let alone a manned space vehicle, was considered absurd. But von Braun believed that it could and would be done. Throughout the course of his career, Werner von Braun saw the launch of Apollo, as well as overseeing the development and implementation of the Space Camp program, allowing young individuals from all over the country to experience just what space flight, travel, and preparation is all about. But von Braun had one simple thought … he had the will to make all his ideas come to be. And so it will be with you, if you believe you can do it. If you have the will, the way will reveal itself.

And this is the basis for beginning the process of making a change in your life. With control, sacrifice, and the will, anything in your life can and will be possible. Use the tools we have provided you here to be a catalyst to begin your journey to change. I have worked with people from all over the country to help them catapult their lives into levels of success they never even dreamed were possible.

And it all began with one small change. Through guidance, insight, and coaching, each of these individuals have been able to not only create lasting change in their lives, but each has also opened their minds to amazing new opportunities and experiences. Let this be the motivation for you to begin your journey to change!

About Jennifer Tuley

As founder and creator of the Breakthrough Success Academy, Jennifer has dedicated her life to not only continually improving her own life, but to helping others create their own remarkable life, as well. Jennifer has successful made two major career changes, each time elevating her life and career to a level of higher performance. As a Manager for Fortune 500 company, Starbucks, Jennifer learned significant leadership skills, which she employees in her personal development coaching today.

Along with serving as developer and implementation specialist for a college technical program, Jennifer works with students on a daily basis to discover their purpose and passion, solidify their skills, and implement them into the workplace. She also currently serves as a strategic liaison to different organizations across the country, providing leadership skills and implementing strategies for management and their teams, allowing them to be more productive and therefore more profitable. The Breakthrough Success Academy is a culmination of Jennifer's life work, bringing together a wide array of thought-leaders, business experts, and strategic alliance partners, all committed to helping others change their lives and seek out their big breakthrough.

Tuley.Jennifer@gmail.com

Starting Fresh

By Gwen Cunningham

"Sometimes when you're in a dark place you think you've been buried, but you've actually been planted."
                               Christine Caine

For years I felt alone. I didn't know who I was, where I belonged, or where I was going. And even worse, I had no one that I felt like I could identify with. I felt as if I was just going through the motions of life. Eleanor Roosevelt said, *"the future belongs to those who believe in the beauty of their dreams"*, but I was too afraid to even attempt to dream about my life or my future.

I was different, and I figured that out early in life. Not only did I stutter, which made me feel alone, but as a young black girl growing up in a predominately white prominent area of Passaic, New Jersey, I always felt like the outsider. By the time I got to middle school, I was teased and picked on, ridiculed as an "Uncle Tom", and accused of talking like a white girl. It was cruel and humiliating and created a lasting impression on me. I felt so alone; not black, not white, just so different. This created a feeling of emptiness inside me that lasted for so many years, like I was never good enough to fit in anywhere.

As I stated, I grew up in New Jersey with my four other siblings – two sisters and two brothers – and my mother and stepfather. And while I felt like I didn't fit in at school, I didn't fit in at home either. My mother regularly told me how I was just like my father, and while most kids would take this as a compliment, I knew that it wasn't. I regularly heard from her how he had mental health issues and everyone thought he was crazy – certainly not traits that I was proud of or wanted to be reminded of.

So while a young girl's safe place should be at home, I was being teased and bullied there, as well as the problems I was having at school. But I didn't go quietly into the night. I fought for my place in the world, maybe not the way I should have, but I did what I felt I could do to protect myself. I quickly developed a swift punch and sharp tongue and used those to fight my way through any difficulty I faced.

Due to my lack of self-confidence, I would continually complain, blame others, and put the responsibility of my actions or my situation on anyone I could, besides myself. I took on the perfect role of the victim. All too often, we build our reality on the foundation of what we see in our environment – both what we've experienced in the past and how we currently see our situation.

I knew that my beliefs determined my attitude and my behavior. Have you experienced this in your life? Have you recognized how easy it is to hold onto mistakes you may have made in the past, long after they have happened? If you're anything like me, I held on to them for years. My mind was filled with self-doubt and negativity. The negative self-talk dialogue going on in my head was so constant and relentless that it blocked any true authentic real conversations from coming through. While on a deeper level, I knew that the "real me" existed, I just didn't know how to get to the place where I could find, connect, and let her come out.

"More people would learn from their mistakes, if they weren't so busy denying them."

Harold J. Smith

While I knew that there was a greater person deep down inside me, I kept listening to the self-doubt and negativity and made some decisions that only supported how I thought of myself. With the struggles I had at home compounded by the fact that I knew I didn't fit in at school, I looked for something to alleviate the pain. By the age of 15 I turned to drugs and alcohol to fill that void and numb the pain. That use and abuse encouraged me to make decisions that I knew my positive true inner self would never have made.

As earlier stated, my family always said how much I was like my crazy father, that self-fulfilling prophecy became true. I found myself in and out of mental institutions throughout my teen years, but never with much success or lasting change, as the drug problem began controlling my life.

Along this destructive path, I made more poor decisions and at age 19 found myself pregnant by a man 17 years older than me. I was so filled with hurt, anger, rejection, and a need to feel like I fit in somewhere. I was looking for acceptance and love in all the wrong places, and finding it in all the wrong decisions. As it was God's will, my son died at birth. It was yet another blow to my feelings of self-doubt and not being good enough. I was desperately struggling to just live.

I knew I needed to make some changes in my life, but not knowing how to do it, I decided to start with a change of scenery. I moved from New Jersey to California with one of my sisters and her family. But just as they always say, no matter where you go you take your problems with you. I tried to make some changes, and it lasted for a little while. I went to college, met some really positive people, and was even able to maintain my sobriety.

I finally felt like I was on my way out of the darkness. But unfortunately, I never dealt with what my issues really were – I just left them in my suitcase and pretended to not unpack them. With all that baggage still there, my insecurities quickly crept back up and I was once again on a path to self-destruction. You see, when we don't actually get to the root of what the issues in our lives are, they will always come back into our lives, no matter what changes we are trying to make or where or how many times we move. Without facing them and working through them, they will always be there.

I was on the road to destruction once again; making poor decisions and allowing the negative self-talk to take control over my actions. In April of 1983 I was gang raped by a close friend and two of his friends. I felt betrayed, hopeless, and violated. I was afraid that I was going to die. That experience brought back the horrible memories of my childhood when I was the victim of incest. I was on a mission of self-destruction. All I wanted to feel was protected and loved. Once again, I knew I needed to make a change, but instead of looking within and working on myself, I moved again. I moved back to New Jersey and on September 23, 1983, I married my high school sweetheart.

Life should have been perfect – a fairy tale, but we were both on the path to self-destruction. He was the only person I wanted to be around, but I could see myself in the same position I was earlier in my life – looking for love in any way possible. I now see how not having my father in my life affected me in so many ways. I was constantly looking for someone to protect me, someone to love me. I realized that I was only looking for that fulfillment within my marriage, and because of that, I knew that it was never going to work out between us. After just a few short months, I told my husband that I couldn't do this anymore and I wanted a divorce. So there I was, off and running again.

Through all this pain, madness, and running, I was so fortunate to have my grandmother in my life. It's amazing how denial works - I didn't realize how my cocaine addiction impacted my life. It took my grandmother to shed light on how my drug addiction had taken over my life. She always saw a greater good for me – one that I couldn't see for myself. Who do you have in your life that is always working for the best for you? Who is always there as that constant force of good for you? For me, it was my grandmother.

In 1985, she came to me and told me about a drug rehab center in New York City. She said that if I didn't go and get my life together, that she was afraid I was going to die. I realized she was probably right. I saw the pain in her eyes, I saw how much she was hurting and how scared she was, but I still did not believe that I had a drug problem. Unfortunately, part of my self-doubt, lack of self-confidence, and self-destructive mindset also adopted the attitude of denial. I spent the next 18 months at the Daytop Village (rehab center...) but I was still in denial as to the extent of my disease and addiction.

I figured out how to work the system and how to adapt. And yet, I still didn't feel like I fit it. I wasn't "one of them". They were all heroin addicts and were living a life constantly in and out of prison, and I just couldn't relate. Luckily, I hadn't gone down that path yet. I continued to work the system and graduated from the program. Upon completion, I was asked to become a counselor for other addicts. I worked my way up and soon became an Assistant Director of the Women's Program. I loved this work. I loved working with other women and helping them to find their own happiness.

I felt like I was really contributing and that finally I was "needed". I was helping to make a difference in their lives, and I was really good at it – taking care of others – but I wasn't taking care of myself. So often, as women, we want to find the place where, not only are we accepted, but we are really needed, and making a difference in someone's life, and I was right there.

From the outside, everything looked great; my family was proud of me, I was helping other women make great changes in their lives, and it looked like my life was great. But as we know, without a mindset shift, the old habits always come back to haunt us. While I looked great on the outside, I was moving closer to death on the inside. I couldn't live with the pain and the hurt any longer and so I started using drugs and alcohol to once again, fill the void. So, on the run again, I picked up and moved several times, crossing the country each time, running as far each time as I could.

"As I unclutter my life, I free myself to answer the calling of my soul."
Wayne Dyer

So this is the place where I found myself; broken, afraid, and sick and tired of being sick and tired. August 21st, 1994. I was carefully planning out every aspect of my suicide. I didn't really want to die, but I just knew that I couldn't live with the pain any longer. It had to stop and this was the only way I could see to make that happen. I was crying out for help. I remember making that phone call to my mother. I told her that I was going to die. She kept me on the phone while she reached out to a friend of mine, begging him to come check on me, knowing what I was planning.

By the time my friend arrived, I had already consumed three bottles of vodka and an array of drugs. He got me to the hospital where they treated me for the overdose, and of course, wanted me to go to rehab. I was furious! I said "hell, no! I've been there, done that! I am NOT an addict!" They didn't understand. I had a great career, my own home, made my own money, had my own car, etc. I tried to convince them that I didn't have a problem, I just needed to get rid of all the "unhealthy" people in my life.

It's amazing how denial works, and just as amazingly how God will put the right people in your life at the right time. My friend Steve was just that person. He owned the company I was working for, and was in recovery also, as well as a few of our co-workers. God was placing people in my life to help me and guide me through this and I didn't even realize it. I managed to get my way out of going to rehab and soon went back to work, scared, emotionally drained, and still detoxing from the weekend.

I remember looking in my bag for something and found a meeting schedule for Alcoholics Anonymous – Steve had hoped I would find it. While looking at it, one of my co-workers came in and saw what I was reading.

He said, "Gwen, do you want to go to a meeting with me at lunch time?" The name of the meeting was Attitude Adjustment, and it sounded like just what I needed. He said, with a smile, "Let's go".

"Transformation is more about unlearning than learning."
Richard Rohr

This was the turning point for my life, my rock-bottom, per se. I went to that meeting that day and every day after that for 5 straight years. Six am Attitude Adjustment, that became my morning routine.

I got a sponsor and started working the famous 12 Step Program of Alcoholics Anonymous. I finally believed that there was a future for me and my life. I had a mindset shift from hopeless to hope.

I found God and he was not the punishing God that I thought he was when I was growing up. I started feeling different, and this time it was from the inside out. I put in the work, and only because I did, did my life begin to change. And so it can be for you as well. As you take one step at a time, hold on to God's hand and let him lead, as He will guide you to where you need to go.

It's Time For A Fresh Start

When I found God, I found everything that I had been searching for; joy, peace, and happiness. I was so blessed to have been given two lives in one lifetime and this was my fresh start. I knew I had a purpose and I was going to let God use me to fulfill that purpose. I took full responsibility for my life and knew that I have the power to reinvent my life and make it whatever I wanted it to be – no more being a victim. I started off by first setting some goals for myself. I had always loved fashion, so I worked tirelessly to fulfill that dream. In 2001, I opened my business, Lady G's Boutique, but that was just the beginning. I knew that my purpose was bigger than just helping people look good on the outside.

I knew that God had bigger plans for me, and everything was finally coming together. I was fulfilling the dream of helping women look and feel amazing. But I still felt like something was missing – I was missing that relationship. I wanted to get back with my husband. I thought that if we could just get back together that everything would now be complete. Unfortunately, during this same period, one of my best friends died and we took in and raised her 16 year old son, Jamal. So now, not only am I trying to raise a young man, but I am trying to balance that with putting back the pieces of a broken marriage. The first year of our new marriage was great, but it didn't take long to realize that getting back into the relationship was a mistake. I was looking to cure the feelings of loneliness, low self-esteem and insecurity, but what I was left with was broken heartedness.

The next 12 years of my marriage life was a downward spiral. I lost myself in my husband and he became my God. My life was turned upside down because I was looking for him to complete me, rather than fixing myself before getting back into the marriage. I spent years of tears and frustration trying to fix what should have been repaired so long ago. Beware of the smooth man that appears as a wolf in sheep's clothing.

I soon found out that my husband's infidelity that he once hid, now became a regular part of our marriage. I was justifying his behavior and actions, covering up for him, and even lying to myself and belittling myself. Once again I found myself at rock bottom. I remember reading a quote that helped me pull myself through. It said:

> **When life knocks you down, try to land on your back because if you can look up, you can get up.**
>
> **Les Brown**

And that's exactly what I did; I took my power back and turned to the only thing that had always been there for me, God. I knew that I had to do the work on the inside first to make the outside what I wanted it to be. I had to get honest with myself and let go of some things so I could finally move on. I knew that I deserved the best. It was time for me to grow up emotionally and let go of the man who was no longer the one who protected me years ago. Therefore I began the process of healing. Truly the best thing that came from this marriage was my son.

I decided that one of the best ways for me to heal was to become a Life Coach. I wanted to work with others to help them take control of their life and have the courage to live their dreams and step out into their destiny. So now I have dedicated my work to the personal development of women who are looking to polish up the image of themselves from the inside and the outside. My philosophy is that your outside cannot shine completely and authentically until the inside is fully illuminated, as well. Whether you are looking for growth and illumination in your career, business, or ministry, my goal is to equip each client with the maps, tools, tips, and strategies to find the treasures inside themselves and discover their best selves.

God had a purpose for my life, to share my story of healing from the inside out, and I have finally accomplished what I set out to do. I did it and I know you can do it too. I overcame the obstacles that lay in my own path and I used my experiences to heal not only myself but others, as well. One of the first things I wanted to do was to write my first book, "The Art of a Fresh Start: A Woman's Guide to Healing From The Inside Out", and during the first two weeks I was an Amazon Best Seller in two categories; self-help and emotions. I'm on my way to doing all that God has in store for me, but what does he have planned for you?

As I conclude this chapter, I would love to share with you the roadmap I've created to help anyone else who may be dealing with similar struggles or obstacles. My hope is that you use this guide to blaze a trail to your new beginning. Welcome to "My Fresh Start".

START WITH AWARENESS

Get Emotionally Honest. To begin the process of healing, you must let go of the desire to numb your feelings, whether it's through shopping, eating, alcohol or drugs. All of these, and so many others simply allow for a distraction to avoid the discomfort, sadness and pain from whatever you are going through. You must learn to mindfully breathe your way through your feelings and emotions. Get honest about the hurt you've caused and/or received and embrace the healing process of authentic forgiveness.

Ponder on what's possible! Avoid the "can't" thinking and other negative language. If you say something often enough, you may start to believe it, so keep your statements positive. Don't be afraid to seek help in accomplishing goals, but remind yourself that you don't need approval from others to recognize your accomplishments. Focus on what you're able to do. Remind yourself of all your capabilities and positive qualities.

Always focus on what you want rather that what you don't want. The mistake that most of us make when we have a problem is talking about it over and over again instead of focusing on the end result and what we want to achieve. Don't talk about it, be about it.

Learn to forgive. Don't hold grudges or other things that are out of your control. Let go of the past and forgive those that have caused you pain. Not only does it cause unnecessary stress, but you will carry the burden on your shoulders rather than letting it go. Turn to God for guidance and let go of the past. Embrace the truth that real beauty is never tangible, but intangible.

START MOVING FORWARD

You are responsible for the overall management of your own thinking. You must confront the reality that certain aspects of your attitude have negative effects on your mindset and could be holding you back from achieving your goals.

Know that every problem comes with a lesson. There is a lesson in everything that happens to us, so we must always be looking for what that lesson is and learn to master it.

"If you make a mistake and do not correct it, this is called a mistake."

Confucius

Rid your life of negativity. If you want to live a positive, joyful life, you cannot be surrounded by negative people who don't encourage your happiness. When I decided to make the change to live a more positive life, I had to rid my life of negative influences. No one is perfect – and perfection isn't the goal when it comes to positivity – but there were people in my life who were consistently negative, who constantly brought me down.

Turn the page. At some point you have to accept that the past has happened and you've done everything in your power to amend mistakes. It's now time to turn the page and accept those events as part of your story, but you don't have to let that story define who you are. They have all contributed to making you who you are.

Be grateful for those experiences, but allow yourself to move on and truly forgive yourself.

List your strengths. This is a simple task that will help you get into a self-positive mindset, which is essential to maintaining confidence.

Look for the positives. There is something good in every person and in every situation. Sometimes you have to look hard to find the good. When I'm faced with a difficult or challenging situation, I think to myself, "what is good about this?" No matter how terrible the situation might seem, I always can find something good if I just take the opportunity.

START TO WIN

Discover your talents and gifts. What is your unique ability, skill, or talent that you truly are passionate about and could provide significant benefits to your family, business, career, community and world at large?

Pinpoint your passions. What do you love to do, that you would do even if you didn't get paid for it? What is it that you just have to do, no matter what?

Major in what matters most. What is the one thing you want to experience, or do, or accomplish, before you die, so that on your last day on earth you feel satisfied and have no regrets?

Pay attention to confirmations. What do other people say you're really good at? People often tell me that they feel better, uplifted, and energized, after spending time talking with me. Not too surprising then, that I now spend my life and even earn my living encouraging others and helping them improve their lives.

Set clear goals. As you build your self-confidence, what are your goals? What would you like to work on? Ask "if this is going to help me learn about myself, whichever way it goes, will it help me develop my self-confidence?" Self-compassion gives us courage and strength to build our self-confidence. It also supports, encourages and empowers us to do what's in our best interests.

Focus only on the things you can change. Start by doing one thing that builds momentum. Momentum creates the positive energy of accomplishment that fuels action in other areas to immediately move on to doing something else, while your energy is high and thriving.

Work on personal and spiritual development. Be willing to surrender and grow. Life is a journey. We are here to learn and love on the deeper level. One step at a time is enough to keep making forward progress. Be patient with yourself. Let go of urgency and fear. Relax and transform striving into thriving.

Make it a habit to meditate. Think on the word of God. Meditating on the word reveals how to act. Your confessions and testimonials of the word and things of God is part of prayer and meditation. When you read, digest and speak the word to yourself.

About Gwen Cunningham-Jones

Gwen is a master at creating focus, bringing out the best in you and propelling you to the next level and it starts right here! She's very passionate about people making that Fresh Start. She has practiced the 12 steps as a way of life since 1994 and mentored other to improve the balance in their lives, set boundaries and grow spiritually for over 19 years before launching her coaching practice. People are drawn to Gwen's spirit.

Gwen's mission has always been to inspire and motivate others to fulfill their potential, pursue their dreams and fulfill their purpose. It starts right here! Coach Gwen's passion has propelled her to bring out the BEST in everyone she's privileged to work with as a Certified Life Coach, Image Consultant, Amazon Bestselling Author and Speaker.

When you join a coaching program with Coach Gwen, you will also gain the proper path to purpose, self-worth, self-identification, personal empowerment and that's just the tip of the iceberg!

Are you ready for your FRESH start?

Contact: *www.freshstartyourlife.com*

Activate Your Faith

By Shavara Lyons

Faith is all you need if you know what you want.

I've always been a firm believer that nothing in life happens to you, it happens for you. As cliché as it may be, always remember to take what was seemingly caused for your harm and use it to your advantage; for everything is designed for an appointed time. How could life be any more wonderful than it already was? Married at age 33 to the man of my dreams uniquely designed for me, mother of the first born son in 25 years on both my mother and fathers side of the family, home owner, entrepreneur, secondary educator for more than ten years, and a plethora of loving family and friends.

Though I've been told that perfect just does not exist I was certain that I must have been as close as I had ever been to it. Things were at an all-time high with the expectation that they would only be getting better. It wasn't until I was faced with adversity that I actually had to activate the faith that I had on reserve that was so deeply buried within me.

My son was only eight months old when my husband and I found out we were expecting once again. We were completely overjoyed and couldn't wait to make the announcement! While most would consider this announcement too soon, we were so excited that our prayers had been answered and nothing could steal our joy. The ideal situation would have been to keep our little blessing under wraps until I was beyond my first trimester, given the cultural superstitions but we were just too excited.

With all that eagerness and anticipation brewing inside me all I could do was eat, sleep, and breathe visions of this new addition and how it would increase the love within our family. **Lucius Annaeus Seneca** said, *"Expecting is the greatest impediment to living. In anticipation of tomorrow, it loses today."*

While lying in bed late one night I awoke to the pain of a thousand knives on my right side.

Not wanting to startle my husband, I began to literally crawl out of bed but was overtaken by unspeakable discomfort, followed by overwhelming fear. I was maneuvering in complete darkness while suffering egregiously in silence. Not even a prayer could escape my lips. After sitting on the throne until it felt as though my back would slip from underneath me, I fell to the floor and began sobbing uncontrollably.

How and why was this happening? The thoughts consumed me. Did red mean blood? Could blood lead to death? Had the worst already happened? How could the temperature in the room possibly get any colder?

My doctor's mouth was moving but I just couldn't comprehend what she was saying; standing before me in this long white laboratory coat, what was she implying? What were these words being spoken by a professional whom I had grown to love and respect; surely not the words that I so desperately never wanted to hear. And then it hit me; while going in and out of mental consciousness those two dreadful words somehow made it through the gate... "I'm sorry," she said." Though I didn't hear another sound, the look on my husband's face spoke more than I could handle. What could possibly make a grown man cry? As I lay with my feet in the stirrups, venerable, and fragile I froze in time. Even as his arms were wrapped around me and his promising words of "we are going to be ok," it just didn't bring me back to life.

Have you ever felt your heart literally ripped out of your chest, leaving you as a complete fish out water gasping for air?

All the encouraging words I had given so many others in their times of need had all just jumped ship, absolutely nowhere to be found.

And so the pity party began.

Was something wrong with me?

Why did my body fail me?

Did I not eat healthy enough?

Was my workout to strenuous?

Was this awful payback for some random sin that I committed in the past?

It's absolutely true that in the midst of our trials most people want someone or something to blame. Staring in the face of defeat I screamed "this was not supposed to happen to me!" Is it safe to say that the very things that give you reason to believe; can make it easy to get discouraged and settle there? I was just looking for answers, answers as to why I had been let down when I had said my prayers, had such high hopes, vowed to be a better me, and made concrete plans to faithfully serve. The vision couldn't be more plain; heck I had even chosen a name. The agony, the grief, and any other emotion used to describe the pain refused to vacate. It just lingered as if it had no other possible place to reside. Defeat has to be the enemy.

Through firsthand experience character is truly designed in toughness, and it just so happens that this was one of the toughest times of my life. If I had only known then that it just wasn't worth it to fight my closed doors. My only regret is that I didn't maintain a "Right Now Faith," a faith that could insure me that the day to day trials and tribulations can be turned around in a moment's notice for the good; a faith I could gravitate toward that would not allow me to waiver from my sense of peace. It's amazing how things change when we put them in the right perspective.

As hard as it seemed and as slow as it felt within 4 months we heard those magical words once again, "You are pregnant!" This was very different than my previous visit, a lot different. I was competent, hopeful, and my restored joy began to ooze through my veins and seep out of my pores.

Smiles and cries... Someone once said that life was about just that; smiles and cries. Well, on this day of so much excitement, expectancy and caution I both smiled and cried. The room at this point was no longer cold. Truth be told, from the way my adrenaline was pumping it felt like a hot summer's day in South Beach, Miami. It was when my husband repeated loud and clear "I told you we were going to be ok," that I actually believed he was right. I needed to commit that no matter what was going to come our way, we were going to be ok.

The Advantage of Disadvantage

Nine months of pure pregnancy bliss is what it was! So grateful for the aches, pains, and the slight nausea, as this was proof that there was life inside of me. Even the mere fact that I had become what I had labeled a *"Toilet Tissue Freak"* didn't bother me. What is a toilet tissue freak you ask? This is the mere act of someone who has had a previous miscarriage with early signs of slight bleeding constantly checking the tissue after urination for possible signs of termination.

Between you and I, during a 4 o'clock am restroom trip a deliriously sleepy me, with eyes half open witnessed slightly pink traces on my tissue following urinating. After crying hysterically, I realized that it was only my shellac nail polish that had seeped through the tissue giving the illusion of a possible risk. Now even I had to laugh at that!

With all going so well the anticipation of my first 3D ultrasound image would take me over the top. As I lay on the bed staring into the monitor with the cool jelly being rubbed on my belly, I began to secretly wonder what exactly could be taking so long to find the babies heartbeat. After minutes that felt like forever the technician began to motion people into the room. Cringing within, the second and third opinions turned into a diagnosis.

What Now! What could possibly be wrong now? *Polyhydramnios* is what they called it. With the most confused look possibly ever given I cried out "but I'm nine months, I'm almost there!" As my eyes welled up with fear, once again the room grew still and cold. I pleaded with the discovery, "but I'm not high risk, "as my voice began to crack from the crocodile tears that I could no longer fight.

Here I resided again in the land of unfamiliar in a far, far away land called "The Unknown." Along with the diagnosis came no real concrete explanation as to what it was (not in layman terms anyway.) The thing that did stick with me was that from day to day my condition could get worse, totally vanish, or remain the same. As if I wasn't paranoid enough already!

Have you ever felt as though you were already dealing with enough in life, and based on the cards you were dealt there was not enough room for more unwanted circumstances to be thrown your way? Can you say, strength finder!"

On January 13th, I was summoned to an overnight stay in the hospital after what I thought was a routine visit with the doctor. While being completely frustrated, I lost the battle of "why can't I go home?" I decided to make a peace treaty with my husband and relax and comply.

There are things in life that we simply may not understand, they may not even make a whole lot of sense in the natural, but there are forces that are working together in the spiritual for our good.

After surviving the night of a perfect storm it was time to be released! What a joyous occasion. I would now be able to go through with the party plans for my son that I was just unwilling to put off. You know those plans that we tend to make without considering nor consulting the chief plan maker? As my husband began to tie my shoes and make a mental note of my 1000th request, the feel of a Rambo knife twisted and repeatedly jabbed me without recourse. Unfortunately, this does not even describe the pain of the contractions I developed out of thin air. My husband called the nurse right away "help!! Someone quick; my wife needs help!!" All I could think of was "is this really happening now? But my son is at school! I don't have my bag! My mother and father are at work! Plus let us not forget I have other plans!"

Who is the Author and finisher of your plans?

Question: If things don't happen the way you desire, is that still not the perfect plan for your life?

The moment of being whisked away to the delivery room is a total blur. While I do not remember the transport, I'll never forget the pain.

So many of us vow to forgive but never forget the pain of a situation, circumstance, or obstacle that we had to face. Moving forward, exactly how many of us have committed to focus on an attitude of expectancy? Know that your life is filled with endless possibility; whether the pain was 2 minutes ago, or 20 years ago…Let it go! You see I allowed my expectations to wavier based on bad news, not enough information, and unforeseen circumstances. I'm sure I'm not the only one who makes plans of how things should be, feels as though my way is the best way, and often is convinced that I should receive a pass that will exempt me from adversity.

While lying in the delivery room I had a placenta abruption, this I could not believe. The placenta – my baby's lifeline to me - had torn away from the inside of my uterus. I just could not understand all the odds. You see things like this happen on TV, but it's not supposed to happened to me! No, rationalizing was taking place as I was rushed immediately into emergency surgery, bright lights for miles and what seemed like a 100 practitioners in the room. I couldn't bring my pulse down long enough to digest what was happening. How much pulling and tugging did they really have to do? And as if we were not afraid enough did my baby really have to come out blue? I remember my husband singing to me, but I also remember how quickly that song was interrupted with the realization that we had to make the decision of a lifetime. "Sir, will you be staying with your wife or going to NICU with your daughter?" They repeated this over and over...

After waking up in the recovery room I was greeted by my mother. It was such a warm feeling having her there. No umbilical cord cutting this time, but blessed beyond measure that she was alive. A healthy baby girl, a scar to show for it, a restored faith, and the will to never give up.

Do you remember a time in your life where your journey was full of so many up and downs? Where it robbed you of your peace and faith of the "Right Now?"

You may not be able to envision how things are going to happen, but that's not your job; your job is to just believe.

Take a Leap of Faith

Sometimes it's through pain, suffering, and agony that we discover that our greatest tragedy has actually lead us to our greatest lesson and blessing.

One would have to truly forgive me for my previous opinions that postpartum depression was a term that was unfit to be considered a diagnosis. See, I use to believe that this term may have been made up in order to justify acts that were totally out of character, or simply used as a scapegoat for unmentionable actions.

After all wasn't this just something that was deemed a nonfictional read or negatively portrayed on television?

How could a chemical imbalance created by such dramatic hormonal changes affect my home in such a way? Me, the career woman, the perfectionist with such high expectations and so many aspirations. Needless to say it turned out that the very thing I chose to judge had now found its way to me. Postpartum robbed me of my smile and allowed all the negative thoughts to become over whelming and severely intoxicating. It was official; the anxiety had kicked in and I desperately needed someone or something to blame.

The emotional roller coaster I was on had me feeling like a real live science fair project. I was relieved to find out that postpartum depression is not due to a personal weakness or a flaw in your character, but even being armed with this knowledge didn't seem to make me feel any better about my current situation. How was I to dig myself out of this little black hole that no one even knew I was in?

Move Forward in Faith

Through it all I grew to understand that my pain proceeded my growth. I'm convinced that you cannot grow without pain. Remember the slogan: "No pain no gain"? Changing my perception helped me to change my life. I began to make conscious decisions to pick up the pieces when the numbness became unbearable. Then slowly the will to be great far exceeded the forces against me.

You can endure anything if you began to understand that the obstacles you face, the heartache you feel, and the pain that penetrates your being can't last forever. Sometimes we find ourselves in a storm that we did not cause. Hear me loud and clear "YOU MUST" wait out the storm!

"But they that wait upon the Lord shall renew their strength."

Know that while you are waiting He will renew your strength; for the joy of the Lord is your strength.

The reality is that as long as we are living, we are going to encounter obstacles. When you are faced with an adversity, make up your mind that you are going to live and not just settle for being alive. I found myself worrying about things far beyond my control, until I realized that we cannot add a single hour to our life by doing so.

The Power of Faith

"Now faith is the assurance of what we hope for and the certainty of what we cannot see, exists." Hebrew 11:1

Stop taking an inventory of everything wrong with you. It amazes me that sometimes we condemn ourselves so much that no one else has to.

Never get discouraged because you don't see relief as fast as you would like. I prayed and asked God to reveal my destiny. In the midst of my despair I asked Him for a revelation regarding the areas of my life that needed more focus and the parts that I needed strength in order to walk away from. Remember were ever it is that you desire to be you can't get there by going backwards. Make a faith driven decision that you will not let minor setbacks keep you from everything major that you have been called to be.

Have you trained your mind to complain, worry, and see the worst? I encourage you to develop an attitude of gratefulness. Find a reason to offer thanks. Train your thoughts to be grateful. As we all know, just when we think things are as bad as they could possibly be, we must realize that they could always be worse. Embrace everyday and accept it as a new day to express your gratefulness.

Let me ask you a question: ***10 years from now will you be more disappointed by the things you believed in that didn't work out, or the things that didn't work out because you didn't believe?*** The mind is so very powerful. When pitiful thoughts consumed me, rational thoughts escaped me. You have to commit to taking every thought under captivity. While two different people can be faced with the very same adversity, their individual perceptions can allow for two radically different realities. I encourage you to "Choose to Change."

Negativity infiltrates your mind with "I'm not good enough" thoughts until you adopt them as your own. Remember, when your negative thoughts consume you defeat has its way in your life.

Generating the Faith Within

Set the foundation that God is about to do something that is going to blow your mind. Boldly decree that the rest of your life undoubtedly will be the best and most amazing days of your life.

I once heard **Joyce Meyers** speak that *"the blessings will come, but the test and trials will most likely to come first."*

So many things tried to destroy my faith. Waking up can be hard to do when you are overly consumed with what you have already declared as defeat. I had to ask myself two very important questions while being 100% honest with myself: Was I responsible for bringing excessive unwanted pain on myself (pity parties, the blame game, the perfect world scenarios?)

and was I purposely living a life of being unfulfilled (pride, resentment, isolation?) Be very leery of taking on the "victim" mentality. Know that everything is not happening to you; it's happening for you.

Sometimes you have to go through to get through. There are going to be many unforeseen things that take place throughout your journey, but do not allow that to interrupt your expectation that great things are going to manifest in your life. Know that there is purpose for your life that will greatly impact the lives of others.

I encourage you to allow your faith to bring you out of those dark places and help you to help others who are struggling in those very same areas. It has been a true blessing to discover my purpose after the pain. Being able to connect with so many that I now have the ability to influence through my experiences in life has given me great purpose. I am convinced that my going through was never meant to harm me but to build me up as living proof for those who don't believe.

It is my belief that there is no influence without experience, and there is no purpose without influence.

It was easy to get discouraged and settle there. I had to trust that the way I went into what felt like a furnace of defeat was not going to be the way that I came out. Never lose sight that the creator of the universe is breaking all barriers in order to get you where you are destined to be. Get in agreement that there is purpose in your pain. Only God knows how to take something that was meant to be a disadvantage and turn it into an advantage.

The words that I simply could not put down, ***"stop living in what was and start living in what is."***

I knew that I was not happy with the negative state of mind that tried so desperately to control me. I knew that if anything was going to change I had to be the one to change it. I began to transition my thoughts as soon as the epiphany hit me that I was either going to stay bitter or I was going to get better.

I told myself over and over again ***"I am a force for good. I am healthy. I am loved. I am more than a conqueror."***

I repeated it in the bathroom mirror, in my car on the way to work, on aisle 9 in the super market, before I went to bed, and as soon as I woke up in the mornings.

I wrote it in my daily planner, on a sticky note attached to my refrigerator, as a reminder in my phone, as a screen saver on my computer, and attached it to anything I frequently laid my eyes on. I evacuated the "stinking thinking" and activated my faith.

The moment my thinking changed, my life changed! Don't avoid your responsibility of change by lying in bed, staying isolated from others, and allowing non activity to overtake you. Trust and believe without a shadow of a doubt that you are healed from your undesirables.

Faith Filled

All that you can see will be given to you. Create a new vision for your life. Don't focus on your problems, whatever you thought was never going to happen is still going to be done. Activate your faith, keep your vision, and rise above your circumstances.

You were not created to be ordinary. Don't allow yourself to be weighed down by the issues of life (depression, self-doubt, who gave up on you, who is not, and what was.) Be assured that everything is going to work out for the good if you just believe!

In those times that you consider less fortunate, never forget to lean not to your own understanding. Even in times where you may want to question the reason you even exist be reminded that things are destined to work out in your favor.

I must confess. I'd absolutely be telling a tale if I didn't admit to going through the "why me?" phase. It's something about feeling as though you have been through enough in your lifetime to even be able to fathom going through anything else. Just as I began to question the misfortune in my life, it was revealed to me that my trials where a part of my story, and my story was pure evidence that all things are possible if you just believe.

My challenge to you is to Rise above, Press beyond, and Go the distance. After all, the creator of us all breaths his life into you.

> *"A belief is only a thought that you continue to think; and when your beliefs match your desires, then your desires must become your reality."*
> **Abraham Hicks**

Don't miss the best parts of your life because you refuse to dream bigger. Do something out of your norm, grow in new ways…make your life fuller! The life destined for you just might require you to **"Activate Your Faith."**

About Shavara Lyons

Shavara Lyons is a dynamic speaker and amazing visionary. She is a firm believer in the idea that if you change your thinking, you can change your life. This philosophy fueled her passion to live life on purpose and pursue a career in counseling, as a life coach, and motivational speaker.

Shavara currently resides in Houston, Texas as a wife, mother, and entrepreneur.

She completed her undergraduate degree in Business at Sam Houston State University which laid the foundation to become the owner of four traditional businesses; always aspiring to serve others.

Shavara is an LPC Intern and holds a dual Master's degree in both Professional Counseling, and Educational Leadership. She is a former secondary educator of 10 years having used this platform to educate, motivate, and instill belief far beyond curriculum. She has counseled and advised many from ages 5 to 85 in both professional, private, and group settings. This is Shavara's first publication of many in an effort to inspire and assist others with realizing everything is within you if you just believe.

www.shavaralyons@gmail.com

Facebook.com/ShavaraLyons

Be True To Yourself

By Dr. Felicia Shaw

I still remember the first gold star I got on my forehead in pre-school. I was so proud; my dress seemed to glow as bright as the star. I fiercely protected the sticker and got to show it off when I got home. Everyone was excited. They seemed so happy and bragged to friends; I felt happy too. They asked me to describe how I received the star and I was thrilled to share the story. That was a "wow" moment in my four-year- old life, and one I never forgot. The feeling was beyond awesome and made me want to do my best at school every day.

We learn to people please at a young age. You receive a star on your paper when you do well, or another accolade. A greater feeling of elation occurs when you make others feel good; almost like a personal high, as if you are walking on cloud nine. But there are times you can go overboard and become an extreme people pleaser. You know, when you do for everyone else and everything else, but not for yourself. That was my story, but let me start at the beginning.

I am the youngest of eight children. The age span between us is 12 years up to 30 years. Because of the age difference, I wasn't close to any of my siblings. All of my brothers and sisters were out of the house by the time I turned five, so I grew up as if I were an only child. I was raised in the city of Detroit by a phenomenal 5 foot tall strong single mom. She had to work to keep food on the table and sometimes one job, became two or three jobs. We weren't "well-to-do", but I never lacked food, shelter or love.

This left me a latch-key child, hanging by myself until mom got home. However, being a latch-key kid, paired with learning from a strong woman, taught me many valuable lessons. Some of those lessons were how to be self-sufficient, take care of business and be comfortable by myself. However, I love to be around people and talk. My mom used to say, "Mouth Almighty, Tongue Everlasting do you ever stop talking". I'm glad I didn't, because who knew, it was a gift.

Lesson 1: Be comfortable being by yourself!

Anyway, when my mom arrived home, I maximized the time to play outside with my friends. To me, everybody was a friend; I didn't have a filter, all I knew is I wanted to hang out with people. People pleasing escalation: I would have given someone my last dime if they asked for it, because that's what you do for friends. I was also easily influenced, but thank goodness I had a healthy respect and reverence for my mom and her rules, so I didn't go too far astray. However, people took advantage of my kindness; we've all been there, where someone takes advantage of your kindness.

I had "so-called" friends who wanted to be friends outside of school and come to my house to hang out, but they bullied me in school. But I learned to deal with it, because I thought this is as good as it gets and I have to take what I am offered.

When those so called friends bullied me, more kids jumped on the band wagon. They allowed me to hang out and took what they could get from me, but picked fights with me in front of others for their personal benefit. I didn't know how to fight back at the time, but I also didn't let this break my spirit. I knew that this life style wouldn't last forever.

Bullies want to silence you. They sometimes want to steal your voice to be in the limelight. However, I was a high-energy child and loved to talk; I'm an extrovert by nature. So I didn't know how to be completely silent. I knew how to downplay myself so that I didn't bring unwanted attention from bullies, but I still had a tendency to slide the last word in.

Nevertheless, my mouth sometimes got me in trouble. Not with anything malicious but it brought unwanted attention. Therefore, I struggled and was bullied significantly in junior high school.

People teased me horribly and told me I was nothing. I didn't let that make me bitter; it made me try harder and want to be better. My mom used to tell me "You can do anything", but the bullies words remained in my head for years. I never felt like I was enough.

Things began to change in high school and I was with a different group of students. Although I experienced bullying, I remained jovial. Remember, I learned to be comfortable by myself and found joy in many things. But as an extrovert, being around people energized me.

In high school, I learned to make people laugh to avoid being bullied. Those things made me feel good as well. I was still a people pleaser who wanted to make people happy and to have them hang around me.

Lesson 2: Never let anyone steal your joy!

People pleasing is a disadvantage, because you can get to the point where you follow others knowing it's not in your best interest. Because you don't want to disappoint, you follow others and end up losing your true self in the end.

The bullying continued in college because I wasn't willing to fight for myself. You see, people pleasing can land you in precarious situations. People might view your generosity as weakness and then take advantage of that weakness. In college I had many people take advantage of me. They did despicable, harmful and cruel things. But after a couple of years, I realized I had a choice to accept this treatment or not; I choose not to any longer. I got tired of being tired.

Lesson 3: You always have a choice!

I had a friend who told me you can't continue to be so open-hearted with everyone because not every person deserves your heart; some people will crush it. Well I got to a point that enough was enough and I closed off my heart. I'm the person who will trust you until you give me a reason not to. Once I'm to the point of permanent distrust, I will close my heart to avoid future hurt from you. I'll forgive, but I won't give my heart back to be misused again. God grants us wisdom.

Lesson 4: Every one doesn't deserve your heart!

For everyone who hurt me, I had to forgive them. Many times people who hurt you will forget about those transgressions but you are left with the pain. To truly begin healing, you need to forgive, which includes forgiving yourself.

You only hurt yourself when you choose not to forgive. It may not be easy, but it's necessary to gain peace of mind. How? Think about the lesson that you can take from that experience. How will you use it to be greater? Don't let the pain of life defeat you or keep you from your destiny.

Lesson 5: Forgive! Let It Go! Use wisdom and move forward!

I met a wonderful man in my senior year of college and he took good care of my heart. We got married a couple of years later and had a child. However, I was still a people pleaser. I love to have my family and true friends around me and making them happy. There's nothing wrong with this behavior except when you leave yourself out of the equation. I did things for everyone else and everything else, but never for me, because I felt I didn't deserve it. The insults of my bullies still swirled around in my head. Do you know anyone who constantly downs themselves? Ironically, I thought I was happy.

Well, in 2005, I moved 400 miles from my family and friends to take a promotion requiring major travel. Although this was a great career move, what followed was one of the hardest years of my life. I was separated from my husband because he couldn't find a job in our new location. So to make ends meet, he stayed with his employer. I felt like a single mom who just happened to be married.

I was four months pregnant and had a four-year-old in a strange place encompassed by a totally different demographic and environment than I was used to. During my third week of living there, I suffered my fourth miscarriage and nearly died. Let me remind you I didn't know anyone in the community. I was taught to be self-sufficient, but I needed help during this time. I had many people come to my aid and I found I wasn't truly alone.

I found people I didn't know had good hearts and were willing to help a stranger. I didn't have to do anything to please them. There are more good folks than the ones who take advantage of you. It was a difficult experience, but I made it with a little help from my newfound friends.

Lesson 6: There's nothing wrong with asking for help, so ask!

Fast forward a couple of months. I remember a co-worker telling me how I represented the Company during my travel time. When you meet with VPs and presidents of other companies, you need to dress like you care. You see, I used to be much heavier, but lost 40 pounds. I still wore large clothes, because I didn't think I needed or deserved new form-fitting clothes. I was in my 30s and I didn't realize that I didn't care about myself. Hmm.

Friends who wanted to show me about self-care, took me shopping and for my first day of pampering; what I difference a day makes. I noticed that when I dressed better, I felt better. Hmmm. And as I began to build relationships and meet people outside the Company, I realized they cared about what I had to say. I was smart enough. I was good enough. I am enough.

Lesson 7: Self-care is a necessity!

After six months I experienced more strife. My toddler was diagnosed with a disorder, I suffered my fifth miscarriage, I lost another sibling, my little protector puppy had to be put down because she got so sick, and my husband was still away because he couldn't find employment in our new location. Our marriage was in trouble. I felt like I had hit rock bottom; I felt so alone.

However, I had to be alone with myself to hear the voice within and know that I could stand on my own. I wasn't what those bullies said about me and I had people who wanted to hear from me. During this time my faith grew stronger and stronger; God was my rock. He was always there providing for me in every situation.

I discovered it was okay to indulge in self-care and love myself; in doing so, I taught others how to treat me. I found out I could be well-respected and not need to be a people-pleaser. As I gave to myself, I was able to give to others from a full cup instead of a dusty one. In that place of loneliness, I found myself and I began to love Felicia.

Lesson 8: You are enough!

When I started to love myself, people noticed I actually began walking differently. I changed my attitude and I began to put new practices in place. This included scheduling time on my calendar for myself, my husband and my son because they're important to me. I learned to balance my life and live with joy from the inside out.

People saw the change and asked me to mentor them and others. I created success tools and began coaching others as well as continually coaching myself. You have to renew your mind on a daily basis.

I discovered my true calling and purpose, which was helping people to live full and balanced lives, uncovering their purpose and walking in it. I do this by speaking internationally, which is operating in my gift. By the way, my mom didn't understand back then why I talked so much, but she is elated my excessive talking emerged into a blessing.

Lesson 9: Uncover Your Purpose!

You are wonderfully made and we were all created for a greater purpose. The hardships you endure are sometimes a wakeup call in life for you to do something greater. Grow from those life lessons. Be amazing. Beginning steps include:

1. Discover who you are and embrace yourself.
2. Learn what's important to you and why.
3. Schedule time for you and your priorities...
4. Journal your Journey.
5. Live Simply in your Purpose!

Lesson 10: You are the final author of your story, be true to you!

My family and I continue to thrive and my faith is even stronger. I'm walking in my purpose. The journey continues to amaze me. I'm grateful for my life and the lessons.

About Dr. Felicia Shaw

As a Balance Expert, Leader of Purpose, certified Life Coach and International Motivational Speaker she empowers high-achieving individuals to gain a sense of their priorities, achieve their goals and simply their lives. Felicia has transformed thousands of people through her successful programs: "The 12 Purposed Protocols of Balance", "Circle of Purpose", and "Purposeful Entrepreneurs".

Felicia is also a Best Selling Co-Author of "Unbreakable Spirit", which is presented by International Speaker, Lisa Nichols. She is also a co-author of "Breaking Free: Overcoming Self-Sabotage". In 2016, Felicia is releasing her newest book, "Conquering the Enemy Within," which teaches on caring for you in 17 minutes a day so you can give effectively to others!

In September 2014, Felicia released her Motivational Audio Book and Inspirational Song, "I Am Enough". It shares how to change your behaviors and maintain a positive mindset. The <u>video of the song, also titled I Am Enough</u>, can be seen on YouTube. Listen to the <u>interview</u>.

She is the radio host of Minding My Business, which provides tips & resources for both aspiring and established entrepreneurs. This show is aired on WXRJ

94.9 FM every Wednesday at 6 pm CST. People can listen to the show on line at www.WXRJ.org.

Felicia received both her BBA and MBA from Western Michigan University. She received her coaching certification from Coach Training Alliance, a school accredited by the International Coach Federation (ICF).

Direct number: 309-706-9615

Direct email: Felicia@SimplyInYourPurpose.com

Website: WWW.SimplyInYourPurpose.Com

My Big Takeaways and Action Items

*Becoming Aware through Love, Health and Loss
By Lisa Marie Martin*

Freedom Fighter: Finding Your Freedom Through Forgiveness
By Patrick Artis

An Unexpected Journey
By Monique Tucker

Staring Stuttering in the Face
By Cicone Prince

The Quiet Storm
By Dr. Nekeshia C. Doctor

A Journey Called Life
By Jennifer Tuley

Starting Fresh
By Gwen Cunningham

Activate Your Faith
By Shavara Lyons

Be True To Yourself
By Dr. Felicia Shaw

Made in the USA
Lexington, KY
05 March 2017